From Afro-Cuban Rhythms
to Latin Jazz

Raul A. Fernandez

D1596101

UNIVERSITY OF CALIFORNIA PRESS

Berkeley   Los Angeles   London

CENTER FOR BLACK MUSIC RESEARCH

Columbia College Chicago

University of California Press, one of the most distinguished
university presses in the United States, enriches lives around the
world by advancing scholarship in the humanities, social sciences,
and natural sciences. Its activities are supported by the UC Press
Foundation and by philanthropic contributions from individuals
and institutions. For more information, visit www.ucpress.edu.

University of California Press
Berkeley and Los Angeles, California

University of California Press, Ltd.
London, England

Center for Black Music Research
Columbia College Chicago

Library of Congress Cataloging-in-Publication Data

Fernandez, Raul A., 1945–.
    From Afro-Cuban rhythms to Latin jazz / Raul A. Fernandez.
        p.   cm. — (Music of the African diaspora ; 10)
    Includes bibliographical references (p.   ) and index.
    ISBN-13, 978-0-520-24707-9 (cloth : alk. paper)
    ISBN-10, 0-520-24707-8 (cloth : alk. paper)
    ISBN-13, 978-0-520-24708-6 (pbk. : alk. paper)
    ISBN-10, 0-520-24708-6 (pbk. : alk. paper)
    1. Blacks—Cuba—Music—History and criticism.   2. Latin
jazz—History and criticism.   I. Title.   II. Series
ML3565.F47   2006
781.64′097291—dc22   2005015752

Manufactured in the United States of America

14   13   12   11   10   09   08   07   06   05
10   9   8   7   6   5   4   3   2   1

This book is printed on New Leaf EcoBook 60, containing 60%
post-consumer waste, processed chlorine free, 30% de-inked recy-
cled fiber, elemental chlorine free, and 10% FSC certified virgin
fiber, totally chlorine free. EcoBook 60 is acid free, and meets the
minimum requirements of ANSI/ASTM D5634–01 (Permanence
of Paper).

CONTENTS

PREFACE

As the twentieth century drew to a close, a small band of elderly Cuban musicians, known collectively as the Buena Vista Social Club, was playing to sold-out concert halls throughout the world, selling hundreds of thousands of compact discs, and starring, with Ry Cooder, in an award-winning documentary by Wim Wenders. They reminded us, not for the first time in that century, that the irresistible rhythms of traditional Cuban dance musics continue to excite audiences everywhere.

To some extent, the success of Buena Vista Social Club was based on the international listening public's familiarity with Cuban popular music forms. By the middle of the nineteenth century, the sounds and rhythms of this relatively small island already exerted a sort of musical hegemony within the Caribbean basin. As early as the 1880s, the *bolero,* known for its passionate love lyrics, was evolving in Santiago de Cuba. It quickly spread throughout Spanish-speaking Latin America, becoming a hemisphere-wide genre. In the 1930s, the rhumba became the rage in the United States and Europe.[1] It traveled to Africa, where it influenced the development of *soukous,* today's most common urban music in sub-Saharan Africa. In the 1940s, another Cuban music genre and dance style, the mambo, spread around the world. In the 1950s, a third dance boom accompanied the development of the cha-cha-cha by Cuban orchestras. Rhumba, mambo, and cha-cha-cha became de rigueur in urban dance halls, spreading Cuban music around the globe.

From the mid-nineteenth century on, Cuban musicians have regaled the world with their spirited creations for dancing: the habanera, the bolero, the *danzón,* the *son,* the rumba, the mambo, the cha-cha-cha, the *pachanga,* the *songo,* and more. As Nuyorican salsa and Latin jazz pianist Eddie Palmieri once said onstage, Cuban musicians have produced "the most complex and exciting rhythms of the planet." One important aspect of Cuban music, in particular the *son* genre, is its capacity to easily absorb elements from other music, mixing them to create new fusions. Thus, in the second half of the twentieth century, the popular dance music of Cuba, in particular the *son,* became the foundation of new synthesis—a mixture of conventional jazz harmonics with the driving rhythms of the Cuban *son*—known as Afro-Cuban jazz or Latin jazz.

The early appeal of Cuban music forms lies in their qualities as fertile mixtures of earlier European-origin instruments, melodies, and rhythms with African-origin instruments, melodies, and rhythms. The high quality of the resulting hybrids has been acknowledged by scholars of music and by artists. Cuba's famed novelist and musicologist Alejo Carpentier called the powerful simplicity of the *son* "an elemental symphony." Distinguished poet Nicolás Guillén took the *son* as the source of many poetic ideas. He penned several books of *son*-inspired poetry that became the centerpiece of the Spanish Caribbean's black poetry movement beginning in the 1930s. From the 1920s on, traveling Cuban musicians took advantage of the obvious popularity of local dance music and sought their fortune playing it in major cities around the world, in Mexico City, New York, Paris, Los Angeles, and Madrid.

Another aspect of Cuban popular music that helped its early spread was its broad similarity to other musics of the Caribbean, such as the Trinidadian calypso, the Dominican merengue, and so forth. Like those neighboring styles, Cuban popular music was truly a people's music, developed by working-class musicians, with lyrics that dealt poignantly with everyday themes of work and play, love and despair. Cuban popular music is sensual; it contains frequent references to food flavors, and it seems driven by the sense of taste: the defining concept for Cuban music is *sabor* (translated approximately as "flavor"), a term that plays a central role in it, much like the term *swing* does for jazz.

It may be misleading to refer to Cuban popular music as simply "dance" music because of its unusual complexity. This quality arises as a consequence of Cuba's felicitous music history. Cuba absorbed and claims as its own several "classical" genres. These include the great vocal traditions of West Africa; the complex drum rhythms of Yorubaland, Calabar, and the Congo River basin; the North African–tinged *cante jondo* of Andalusia, Italian opera, Spanish zarzuela, and European art music and ballet. Cuban popular singers intone melodies in manners that may recall old African chants, Spanish flamenco, or Italian bel canto. For the last two centuries, leading Cuban musicians have included master drummers in the Afro-Cuban tradition as well as musical creators in the Western European art music style, from baroque composer Esteban Salas in the early nineteenth century to Leo Brouwer today, and superb performers from nineteenth-century violinist Brindis de Salas to contemporary guitarist Manuel Barrueco. The various styles of music performed by these musicians were never completely separated in Cuban culture: many musicians expertly trained in European classical music forms nevertheless were active as composers and players of popular dance music.

Thus, several centuries of interaction between musicians and audiences from diverse backgrounds in Cuba have produced one of the most intricate and appealing dance musics of the world. A media critic, after attending a concert by Cuba's famed dance band Orquesta Aragón, summarized his impressions in this way: "The layered rhythms, oddly placed accents, perpetually changing instrumental textures and unexpected stops and starts indicated Orquesta Aragón was playing dance music of a higher order than the term usually suggests."[2]

There is a growing body of literature on Cuban music and Latin jazz. Yet much remains to be done. For example, there is no in-depth monographic study of the Cuban *son* or of the origins of Latin jazz in the United States and Cuba. The chapters that make up this volume constitute a small contribution to the growing literature on those subjects. The unifying focus of these chapters has been, for the most part, not the musical styles per se but the musicians that created and developed them. I have grouped the chapters into two parts, Part I (chapters 1–3), focused on issues of social and historical musicology, and Part II (chapters 4–8), made up of biographical essays on eight prominent Cuban musicians.

A brief introduction, "Popular Music," excavates the connections of Cuba to other Caribbean countries with different languages and histories by looking at musical links between Caribbean nations—Colombia, Cuba, Haiti, Puerto Rico, and so forth—grounded in a shared history of revolutions, social upheavals, and labor migrations. Chapter 1, "The Salsa Concept," examines the rise of the salsa music movement in the United States, its evolution and maturation. Chapter 2, "Ontology of the *Son*," examines the history and development of the *son* genre in its various manifestations: as a dance, as poetry, and as instrumental form. The most influential of Cuban dance music styles, the *son* belongs to that select group of New World musics, which also includes the blues, jazz, tango, and samba, that revolutionized twentieth-century music. Chapter 3, "The Aesthetics of *Sabor*," examines the ways in which Cuban popular musicians in the twentieth century developed a characteristic manner of approaching and playing dance music, constructing an entire aesthetic around the defining concept of *sabor*.

Part II begins with a brief introduction, "On the Road to Latin Jazz," a title alluding to Jack Kerouac—a poet who loved Afro-Cuban jazz—that contextualizes the section's biographical chapters. Afro-Cuban jazz emerged in the United States as part of the bop revolution. With the advent of bop, jazz moved away from the commercialism that plagued the genre in the 1930s. Bop musicians sought to establish jazz as an abstract genre not tied directly to dancing. Paradoxically, Cuban music was undergoing a revolution of its own—led by musicians such as Israel "Cachao" López and Arsenio Rodríguez—that increased its appeal to dancers. Afro-Cuban jazz was the result of the fusion of these two irresistible forces. Chapter 4, "Magic Mixture," describes the accomplishment of Cachao ("the best bassist in the planet," according to Jaco Pastorius), whose recordings are a veritable clinic for students of both Cuban dance and Latin jazz traditions.

The next two chapters are devoted to five foundational percussionists of modern Cuban music and Latin jazz. Chapter 5, "Drumming in Cuban," is a study of "Mr. Watermelon Man," Ramón "Mongo" Santamaría, whose work with Tito Puente, Cal Tjader, and his own band made the conga drum a ubiquitous instrument in U.S. popular music. The conga, known in Cuba as *tumbadora,* is a Creole drum developed in Cuba from central and West African predecessors. Chapter 6, "Lords of the *Tambor,*" recounts the percussion exploits of a set of individuals who, together with Mongo, laid the rhythmic basis for the growth and development of Latin jazz between 1950 and 1990: "Hands of Lead," Armando Peraza; Patato Valdés; Francisco Aguabella; and "The Candy Man," Cándido Camero. Chapter 7, "Chocolate Dreams," looks at a leading melody instrumentalist in the Cuban *son* tradition, Alfredo "Chocolate" Armenteros. The last chapter, "The Taste of *¡Azúcar!*" looks at the career of a female vocalist who, in an artistic world dominated by men, led the way in the internationalization of Cuban dance music: the late "Reina Rumba" and "Queen of Salsa," Celia Cruz.

My goal in grouping these essays together is to introduce the reader to the complexity and richness of Cuban dance music and to the thick webs that connect it, historically and socially, to other Caribbean musics, to Latin jazz, and to salsa. While there have been some excellent, and ambitious, attempts at *general* comparisons between various musics of the African Americas, I believe that such studies still suffer from the absence of more detailed histories, empirics, and the aesthetic theorizing of *particular* national genres outside the United States and in non-English-speaking nations—namely, the Cuban *son,* the Brazilian samba, and so forth. In this work, I hope to contribute to a historical, biographical, and theoretical platform on Cuban music that may serve others who wish to establish richer comparisons between different national forms and eventually develop a more encompassing regional aesthetics. Put another way, my approach is more in keeping with Benítez Rojo's attempt in *The Repeating Island* to identify (musical) specificities than with a discussion of commonalities à la Paul Gilroy's in *The Black Atlantic.*

Thus, I utilize a set of terms and definitions that I hope might allow people to discuss Afro-Cuban music and Latin jazz in a conceptual and theoretical manner. I also highlight the work of a number of musicians who, perhaps with the exception of Celia Cruz, were never musical celebrities but rather journeymen musicians who labored for decades in relative obscurity. The fact that among the eight musicians chosen are five drummers and one bassist is not accidental: on the shoulders of these, and a myriad of other "rhythm musicians," Cuban dance music has been and continues to be built.

I have maintained an intense interest in, love of, and respect for Cuban music and Latin jazz since I was a child. I was born in the province of Santiago de Cuba at the eastern end of the island, a region that gave birth to the *son* and the bolero. I grew up surrounded by the sounds of the drums of carnival and Afro-Cuban religious festivities. After coming to the United States in the early 1960s, I earned a PhD in political economy and, in the early 1970s, began teaching in the School of Social Sciences at UC Irvine. Along the way, I became an amateur percussionist and played conga drums, first in the San Francisco Bay Area, where I performed with small dance bands in various East Bay Puerto Rican community clubs, and later in the Los Angeles area, where I played in informal rumba and percussion sessions over the years. I also collected

Afro-Cuban music and Latin jazz recordings, read voraciously about the music and its musicians, danced to the music wherever and whenever I had a chance, and educated myself broadly about my homeland's performance traditions. Beginning in 1975, trips to Colombia in pursuit of my research in political economy opened up new vistas about Afro-Caribbean music. My love for the music sustained me intellectually and emotionally over the many years when travel to Cuba has been difficult and sometimes impossible.

About fifteen years ago, I developed several courses in Cuban popular music and Latin jazz at UC Irvine at both the undergraduate and graduate levels. In the mid-1990s, my interests, pleasantly and unexpectedly, flourished. I was hired as a consultant by the Smithsonian Institution Jazz Oral History Program. That association afforded me an opportunity to interview at length more than a dozen major Latin jazz, Cuban, and salsa musicians and to research their work and contributions. Conversations with these musicians in New York, Los Angeles, Miami, San Francisco, Havana, and Santiago de Cuba reinforced my insights and built confidence in my understanding of the music. Later I agreed to curate an exhibit, *Latin jazz: La combinación perfecta,* sponsored by the Smithsonian Institution Traveling Exhibition Service, which opened in Washington, D.C., in October 2002 and that will travel to twelve U.S. cities through 2006. As part of that project, I authored a book of the same title which accompanies the exhibit and co-produced for Smithsonian Folkways Recordings a CD of classic Latin jazz tunes.

For all of my adult life I have maintained a passion for Cuban music and Latin jazz and educated myself in these realms at every opportunity. This work is the product of that enduring passion and my lengthy but unfinished education.

I would like to thank many people who made this book possible, especially those whom I had the privilege of interviewing for the Smithsonian Jazz and Latino Music Oral History Projects. The concepts developed in Part I owe a great debt to my conversations in Havana with Frank Emilio Flynn, Richard Egües, Tata Güines, Luis Carbonell, Félix Guerrero, Antonio "Musiquita" Sánchez, and Celina González; and in Santiago de Cuba with Enrique Bonne and Rodulfo Vaillant. Part II of the book would have been inconceivable without the memories and observations of Israel "Cachao" López, Mongo Santamaría, Armando Peraza, Francisco Aguabella, Chocolate Armenteros, Patato Valdés, Cándido Camero, and Celia Cruz. Formal interviews and many informal conversations with Chucho Valdés, Bebo Valdés, and Carlos del Puerto helped round out some ideas about the development of Cuban music and the origins of Latin jazz. Special thanks go to musician and musicologist Anthony Brown, who opened the door for me to conduct all of those interviews. A number of profoundly musical individuals have taught me more about the practice of music than they realized, among them legendary bassist Al McKibbon; flutist nonpareil Danilo Lozano; musicologist and all-around scholar Katherine Hagedorn; the late, great bassist and *tresero* Humberto Cané; and historian and excellent spouse of mine, Nancy Fernandez. In Havana, Radamés Giro and Leonardo Acosta have been a constant source of inspiration and knowledge about Cuban music and jazz. In Bogotá, Colombia, my comrades Héctor Valencia, Enrique Daza, and Carlos Naranjo provided me with political guidance and infused me with musical enthusiasm. Rafael Bassi, in Barranquilla, Colombia, supported me with his encyclopedic knowledge of Caribbean music. Arthe Anthony taught me a thing or two about the history and culture of early New Orleans. From Roque Morán, who had played and studied with one of the masters, Arsenio Rodríguez, I learned as much as I could about the complexity of the *son montuno*. I could never learn all the things that *bongosero* extraordinaire José Antonio Asseff has shown me on his bongo. Mariano Sánchez has been my greatest advisor and supporter when it comes to digital technology. Enid Farber and Mark Holston allowed me access to their great photographic resources. Viredo Espinosa gave me carte blanche to look through his great artistic production in search of a suitable design for the book dust jacket. Monica Giannini took charge of preparing the final manuscript for submission. I am immensely grateful to Mary Francis, Music and Film Editor at the University of California Press, and to her assistant, Kalicia Pivirotto, for navigating the manuscript through the (to me) unexplored ocean of UC Press publication procedures. Finally, I wish to thank Jimmée A. Greco for an outstanding copyediting job and Rose Vekony for all of her support during the editing process.

PART I

Popular Music

Worksong of the Caribbean

> The lyrics are rarely deep and often bawdy: at least half the songs are
> about sex. But they have the richness of colour, rhythm and dialect
> that marks out the best of Caribbean poetry.
>
> —Gregory Salter, "The Loudest Island in the World"

The question of whether there is an underlying unity to the Caribbean
region has been a conundrum for many scholars. The people of the Caribbean basin—all the Antilles and some of the continental coastal areas that shape its perimeter—are usually characterized by their diver-
sity: their languages, history, natural environment, cultural expression,
political boundaries, and so on. Students of Caribbean literature bow to
language differences by neatly separating Caribbean expression into
the Anglophone, Francophone, and Hispanophone areas. Important
historical records of the region are dispersed in repositories in Spain,
France, England, and Holland, making it difficult for researchers to
determine historical commonalities.[1] Access to the music of the region,
however, is not quite so difficult. We can cautiously argue that while
borders may separate people, music nevertheless tends to unite them.

The quotation at the beginning of this introduction—a description
of a Caribbean popular music genre—could apply to any number of
forms. It might refer to calypso, salsa, *son,* meringue, or *mento.* It points
to the common aspects of the popular musics of the basin, which share
many rhythmic patterns, instrumental formats, and styles.

Louis Moreau Gottschalk long ago recognized the unifying themes
of Caribbean music. Born in New Orleans in 1830, this gifted American
composer and pianist came from a family that became split by the revolution in Haiti. Some members remained in Haiti and served in the new
independent republic; his maternal grandfather and his mother—an infant at the time—moved first to Jamaica and later relocated to New Orleans. As a child he was exposed to the melodies and rhythms of Haiti,

sung to him by his nanny, a black slave woman who had been brought along by his family from Saint-Domingue. As we shall see, this woman whose name we do not know was perhaps one of the most influential individuals in the history of the development and diffusion of Caribbean music.[2]

Gottschalk's virtuosity at the piano took him to France at an early age and later to Spain. Beginning in 1854, he took a series of trips to several islands in the Caribbean. Over the next ten years, he visited Trinidad, Haiti, Martinique, and Puerto Rico and lived for extensive periods in Guadeloupe and Cuba. During his travels, Gottschalk encountered the same sounds he had first learned as a child in New Orleans. He absorbed this music with passion and wrote numerous themes based on the music of Puerto Rico, Cuba, and Guadeloupe. Far from being a "culture cannibal," Gottschalk promoted and helped local musicians wherever he went and became a close friend and collaborator of the leading musicians of the area. Gottschalk organized orchestras and concerts in city after city in the "repeating islands" of this Mediterranean Sea. On one occasion, he organized a concert in Havana with hundreds of musicians, including a team of more than forty percussionists from Santiago who were paid to travel six hundred miles to the west. At this megaconcert, the orchestra performed his *Night in the Tropics* symphony, composed some time earlier during a one-year retreat in Guadeloupe. The Bard of the Tropics, as he came to be called, wrote numerous *contradanzas,* and his works are peppered with the sounds of the tango and the *cinquillo.*[3] Through his work, the common sounds of the Caribbean were further diffused throughout the area, even to islands that he never visited. Gottschalk's compositions, it has been reported, were among the best-selling music in the major music store in Curaçao in the late nineteenth century.[4]

What explains Gottschalk's wide-ranging musical repertoire and popularity? Was he unique? And what might he tell us about national and transnational cultural patterns in the Caribbean region?

I would say that the development and diffusion of Caribbean musical modes owes also to the economic conditions of life throughout the region: the interregional migration of labor and, especially, the work of slaves or wage laborers in sugarcane fields and on coffee farms. The corpus of Caribbean genres—*son, mento,* calypso, meringue, *bomba,* and so forth—can be seen as the distinct, national worksongs of the entire region, created by the same people whose muscle, nerve, and sweat supported the fabric of these different yet similar societies.

The legendary settlement of the Palenque de San Basilio, near the city of Cartagena on the Caribbean coast of Colombia, illustrates how music and the people that make it and share it can transcend geographical distance and political boundaries. The entire Atlantic littoral of Colombia, from Barranquilla to the Gulf of Urabá, witnessed numerous and extensive rebellions by African slaves in the seventeenth and eighteenth centuries, which led to the formation of independent communities, or *palenques.* The present community of San Basilio dates its inception to a successful slave insurrection that took place in the first years of the seventeenth century. The *palenqueros* successfully fought off attacks by the Spaniards, who agreed to grant them autonomy in 1603. Further attempts by colonial authorities to regain control failed until, in the early 1700s, the Spaniards were forced finally to ratify local autonomy.[5] San Basilio remained fairly autonomous until increased economic relations with the outside world began to encroach upon the settlement in the early twentieth century.

In the 1920s and 1930s, the music of the Cuban *son* spread by way of recordings and films throughout Latin America. The *son* took root in numerous areas of the Atlantic coast of Colombia, aided by the migration of Cubans connected to the production of sugarcane to the area. Local *sextetos* and *septetos de son* soon developed. In Palenque de San Basilio, a *sexteto* was formed in the 1930s that remains active to this day. The repertory of these groups is essentially the *son* and the *bolero-son*. The instruments in these *sextetos* match those common to Cuban groups: claves, maracas, guitar, bongos, and so forth.[6]

A number of factors help explain how and why the Cuban *son* was so readily adopted on the Colombian coast. The rhythm of the music was carried—like much African-derived musics—on skin drums played by hand. Popular commercial films showed the Cuban musicians to be largely blacks and mulattoes, like much of the population of the Atlantic littoral and unlike the people from the Colombian highlands. The lyrics were sung in a Caribbean Spanish closer to the local dialect than the sound of highland Colombian Spanish. The songs spoke of work in the cane fields and of eating poor people's staple foods such as cassava and plantains. In short, the music contained musical and cultural elements for which coastal people could feel a strong affinity.

We can surmise that in spite of, or rather because of, its Cuban origin, this music—together with its characteristic instruments and repertory—came to be adopted as a local traditional form on the Colombian coast. *Son* and *bolero-son* are included as such in Colombian anthologies of regional folklore. Common historical and musical roots and affinity also explain why in recent years the Atlantic coast of Colombia has also contributed greatly to the developing sound of salsa—a hybrid of Cuban, Puerto Rican, and other musics from the Spanish Caribbean. Thus, in the Colombian Caribbean coast, we witness the peaceful coexistence of national and transnational musical identities, simultaneously Colombian and Cuban.

Caribbean music has traversed not only political borders but linguistic boundaries as well. In the late 1700s, the greatest of all *palenquero* rebellions took place in the French colony of Saint-Domingue. This movement culminated in the creation of the first independent republic of Latin America and led, as is often the case during revolutionary times, to an exodus that involved every stratum of the population. Sugar and coffee planters and slaves, as well as free peasant and working-class blacks and mulattoes, scattered, and the musical and cultural ripples connected to this event are still being felt, sometimes in surprising ways, throughout the sea of the Antilles and beyond.

Some of the French-speaking planters fleeing the Haitian independence movement went to Spanish Puerto Rico, where they set up plantations to continue the cultivation of sugarcane and coffee. Today on the island of Puerto Rico there exists a musical form, a drum, and a

Example 1. *Cinquillo*

Example 2. *Bomba* composite rhythm (two or three supporting drums)

dance all known as the *bomba,* which, in the last fifty years, came to be regarded as one of the most characteristic expressions of the national folklore. The structure of the traditional or folkloric *bomba* is held together by a rhythmic pattern—known as *cinquillo*—played by sticks on a wood block, although this is not always done in modern orchestrations of this rhythm (exx. 1 and 2). Researchers who have investigated the historical roots of the *bomba* drums and dances have all agreed the rhythms played on these drums were performed by slaves and free black workers who were brought, or who came on their own, to work on the Puerto Rican island following Haitian independence.[7]

Bomba established a Puerto Rican national tradition as well as contributed to the development of transnational salsa. The *bomba* became part of mass popular music in Puerto Rico due largely to the work of bandleader Rafael Cortijo in the 1950s. It worked its way into salsa especially in compositions by Nuyorican bandleader Willie Colón. In 1994, two hundred years after the beginning of the Haitian revolution, a Grammy Award was given in the United States to the Cuban American singer Gloria Estefan for her CD *Mi tierra*. The *bomba* rhythm—so closely associated with Puerto Rican folklore—may be heard behind the title song, with its lyrics that speak repeatedly of Cuban themes, Cuban traditions, and the general nostalgia of Cuban Americans for their island homeland.

The historic-musical record can help unravel this interwoven cultural fabric. More or less simultaneous with the Haiti–Puerto Rico migration, another inter-Antillean migration occurred. A broad group of fleeing Saint-Domingue planters, along with their slaves, free black peasants, and employees, resettled in the old province of Oriente in eastern Cuba. There the transplanted planters began coffee production, especially around the cities of Santiago de Cuba and Guantánamo. There, too, a musical tradition developed in communities of slaves, free black peasants, and workers based upon the drums, rhythms, and traditions brought over from Haiti. The music played at these *sociedades,* some of which are still active in Santiago and Guantánamo, is known as *tumba francesa.*

The *tumba francesa* contains rhythmic figures and a "feel" that became part of Cuba's musical heritage (ex. 3). Its drums, drumbeats, and percussive figures on accompanying sticks are similar to those of the Puerto Rican *bomba.* In the orchestral arrangements, the bass lines of the *bomba* and the Cuban *montuno* follow the same pattern. These musical clues, based on historical events, can help decipher the conundrum of why, as in the case of Gloria Estefan's interpretation of "Mi tierra," a tune based on a "Puerto Rican" rhythm of "Haitian" ancestry could resonate so strongly among Cubans. It constitutes another example of the multifaceted Caribbean sensibility. The tune could be identified— depending on the audience—as either Cuban or as belonging to a pan-Latino genre that includes Spanish-speaking peoples from all regions of the Caribbean.[8]

Direct memories of the politico-economic exodus from Haiti have long receded. Yet, as the above examples suggest, a collective musical memory remains. This cultural inheritance originating in the music of some of those who migrated from the French colony continues to influence the popular music of the entire Spanish-speaking Caribbean to this day.

The irony is that people who fled the movement for national independence in Haiti helped preserve, albeit unwittingly, musical forms

Example 3. *Tumba francesa*

that would evolve to symbolize notions of independence and national identity among other Antilleans. The development of the genre known as the *danzón* constitutes a particularly telling example of this irony and exemplifies the continuing cultural impact of the Haitian revolution and the migration that followed in its wake.[9]

A year after Gloria Estefan's *Mi tierra* received a Grammy, the first Grammy awarded under the category of Latin jazz went to a CD entitled *Danzón (Dance On)*. A few years before, a Mexican film also called *Danzón* had won a number of international awards.[10] The genealogy of the *danzón* and its characteristic rhythmic patterns provide a road map of the ways in which music in the Caribbean evolved as working musicians traveled through language and political barriers.

In the 1700s, "society" dance in the Antillean colonies was dominated by the European *contredanse*. The origins of this form are somewhat obscure, but most authors trace it to the English "country dance" of the seventeenth century. The form provided inspiration to a number of European art music composers, notably Mozart. In the eighteenth century, *contredanse* became the favored dance in European courts and salons, thereby making it obligatory for the elite planter society in the colonies to follow suit. The *contredanse* in Saint-Domingue and Cuba, the two major European colonies in the Caribbean in the eighteenth century, was modified in its interpretation by working musicians—mostly black and mulatto—whose reinvention creolized the form.[11]

The settlement of wealthy planters from Saint-Domingue in eastern Cuba in the early 1800s provided an impetus for musical activities in that area. All over Cuba, French was the prestige language of the salons, and things French commanded respect and adulation in elite circles. The creolized version of the *contredanse* imported from Haiti would fuse

Example 4. Habanera (ancestor of tango)

with and reinforce the local *criollo* version over the next several decades.[12] Rhythmic cells such as the tango, habanera, and *cinquillo* became dominant patterns in the newly emerging styles (ex. 4).

This evolution led to the development of the Cuban *contradanza,* a form that "exuded sensuousness,"[13] and later, in 1879, the *danzón,* a couples dance regarded as the first truly "national" Cuban dance genre. Thus, one hundred years after the anti-independence planter elite brought the *contredanse* out of Saint-Domingue, its descendant, the *danzón,* had become identified with the Cuban independence movement against Spain.

These musical genres did get around. The *contradanza*—in particular the rhythmic figure known as the tango or habanera beat—was an important component of early jazz. Composer and pianist Jelly Roll Morton pointed to this rhythm when he declared that in the early jazz of New Orleans (a Caribbean city), there was always a certain "Spanish tinge." W. C. Handy used the tango beat in his "Saint Louis Blues." The heir to the *contradanza,* the *danzón,* spread quickly. In 1881, two years after it was first composed in Matanzas, Cuba, *danzón* sheet music was for sale in music stores in New Orleans. *Danzón* took root in Mexico at the beginning of the twentieth century, where it became part of the local heritage in another Caribbean city, Veracruz. It became the "society" dance of choice throughout the Spanish Caribbean in the first half of the century.[14]

We must note that rhythmic cells characteristic of the *contradanza* and the *danzón* are also present in other Caribbean dance genres, namely the merengue in the Dominican Republic and the calypso in Trinidad. These various styles arose probably as a combination of inter-Caribbean diffusion resulting from multiple inter-island labor migrations and independent developments from common roots.[15] They became differentiated over time as local musicians infused basically similar rhythms with a different feel, varying cadences, tempos, and local melodies.

Diffusion of already similar instruments, styles, formats, and rhythms has continued in the twentieth century. Musicologist Kenneth Bilby tells us, for example, that "in its original form, played in the eastern part of Cuba, the *son* sounds rather similar to *mento* as played by a Jamaican string band."[16] Bilby also finds "Cuban influence . . . suggested by the frequent use of what is called a 'rumba box' in Jamaica."[17] Conversely, other scholars have pointed to the presence of Jamaican-style drums and terminology in popular music and instrumentation in eastern Cuba. A prominent *comparsa* of Santiago's carnival features a *toque de Obía,* strongly suggesting an allusion to Jamaica's *obeah.*[18]

These cultural links should not come as a surprise. Maroon communities, independent contraband commerce, and the development of creolized centers fairly removed from colonial control were centered in areas of Haiti, the north coast of Jamaica, and eastern Cuba for centuries, allowing for extensive contact and interaction among the peoples of the region.[19] In the late nineteenth and the first half of the twentieth century, Jamaican workers were, legally and illegally, imported to work in eastern Cuba in the cane fields and as domestic servants in cities such as Santiago and Guantánamo. For several decades, this labor force traveled back and forth between the two islands, with unavoidable cultural exchange by-products.

In the late nineteenth and the early twentieth centuries, a much larger migration of workers went from Haiti to Cuba to labor in cane fields and coffee farms in old Oriente province. Haitian celebrations, such as the Easter *rara* parades, instruments, and religious practices took root in rural areas of eastern Cuba.[20] The Cuban *son* became popular in Haiti via return migration and radio broadcasts.

By the 1950s, important exponents of Cuban popular dance music were traveling to Haiti for long performance engagements: singer

Celia Cruz, trumpeter Chocolate Armenteros, percussionists Rolando LaSerie and Cándido Requena, pianists Peruchín Jústiz and Bebo Valdés, and many others. The foremost rhythmic pattern in Cuban music, the clave, found its way into the Haitian meringue, which, like the old Jamaican *mento,* sometimes became nearly indistinguishable from its cousin across the Windward Passage. In the last twenty years, diffusion of music across language barriers has become institutionalized by way of various festivals that feature Anglophone, Francophone, and Hispanophone popular musics.[21]

Popular music has allowed some Caribbean people both to enjoy a national identity in their respective countries and to share a common identification with musics from nearby and distant regions within the basin. An interwoven social history and the development of national popular music styles inform one another: the social history of migration helps explain cultural patterns and shared sensibilities, while musical history and forms illuminate cultural agents of change and identity formation. The history and evolution of popular music provides a running commentary to centuries of slavery and wage work, in cane fields or in coffee farms, in rural areas and in the cities. Caribbean popular music can be interpreted as an overarching musical riff, a repetitive worksong that helps tie us together and interrelate a set of revolutions, economic changes, and labor migrations spanning five centuries.

CHAPTER ONE

The Salsa Concept

An analysis of the music forms known collectively as salsa provides a good starting point for the study of Cuban music. Beginning in the 1980s and 1990s, musical styles from the Spanish Caribbean based largely on Afro-Cuban traditions enjoyed a boom in the United States. Performers such as Celia Cruz, Rubén Blades, and Eddie Palmieri received music awards. Films such as *Cross Over Dreams* (1984), *Fatal Attraction* (1987), and *The Mambo Kings* (1992) featured salsa dance bands. In the United States, this type of music had undergone several periods of development, from initial enclave status through sporadic cases at "crossover" to the new, increased popularity.[1]

The styles involved are for the most part dance musics—the result of African, European, and to a lesser extent Amerindian and Asian contact. Dancing has been inseparable from Afro-Latin music in all of its manifestations, from the centuries-old ceremonies of Afro-Cuban religions to contemporary Nuyorican salsa tunes.

Salsa is a collective term of recent vintage that encompasses several Afro-Latin musical forms. It replaced the older *Latin music* term and is accepted only begrudgingly by traditionalist musicians. For some, salsa is nothing but Cuban dance music. Others emphasize the Puerto Rican influence in the development of the style.[2] Musically speaking, the core

13

of salsa stems from the Cuban turn-of-the-twentieth-century country style, a marriage of southern Spanish and West African forms known as the *son*.

The *son* and its descendants were readily accepted in surrounding areas because they did not appear "foreign" to local musicians. In addition, along with the Cuban *son,* related styles had simultaneously developed in Puerto Rico, Colombia, and Panama, such as *seis, porro,* and *tamborito.* As elaborated later on by largely Nuyorican musicians, salsa developed by acquiring other elements from Puerto Rico, Venezuela, Colombia, the Dominican Republic, Panama, and other regions of the circum-Caribbean as well as from American jazz. Salsa musicians old and young attest to the centrality of Cuban dance music in the salsa phenomenon. Thus, Dominican Johnny Pacheco and Nuyorican Jimmy Bosch call Cuban music the "seeds of salsa" and the "main threads of salsa," respectively. Yet salsa cannot be limited to a musical definition. It became identified with Latino urban communities in New York and other U.S. cities as well as cities in the Caribbean. Recognition of this extramusical character is implied in the various descriptions of it given by musicians, for example, Willie Colón, who says that "salsa is a concept"; Rubén Blades, who calls it "the folklore of the cities"; and Celia Cruz, who referred to it as a "working people's music."

AFRO-LATINO DANCE FORMS
IN THE UNITED STATES

Afro-Latino musical styles have been part of the U.S. musical scene for decades. To use one example, the late New York–born Tito Puente recorded more than one hundred LPs and CDs from 1950 to 2000. Regardless its exact origins, the new variant known as salsa began to enter the U.S. popular music scene in a substantial manner in the 1970s and 1980s. Under this new name of salsa, genres previously known as *mambo, son montuno, guaracha,* and *bomba* enjoyed a boom, centered in New York as well as the Caribbean. Afro-Latino genres developed side

Example 5. Clave (*son clave*, 3–2)

by side with the evolution of American music, including jazz, throughout the twentieth century. A continuous exchange characterized this parallel development: American music has repeatedly borrowed from Spanish-Caribbean traditions and vice versa. But in many ways the growth and development have been independent. Elements maintaining the separation include matters of convention in the construction of national musics, language differences, and musical intelligibility.

The frequent exclusion of this music from the canon of American music reflects a tradition in national music histories which privileges genres that come from the local, rural folk, or at least "the bottom up," hence the conventional inclusion of every form of modern African American music as well as Native American and even *norteño* forms. Afro-Latino styles, on the other hand, are perceived by many as transplanted urban musics that fall outside the boundaries of the imagined national music community.

Aside from this quasi-academic exclusion, other elements are involved in the distance that separates salsa and all Afro-Latino styles from "American" music. Language difference constitutes the most obvious impediment. Other obstacles are of a musical kind. Americans historically had difficulty understanding how Afro-Cuban and Spanish-Caribbean music is played, as did Latin American musicians and audiences from outside the Caribbean. First, arrangement and improvisation in much Afro-Cuban music and, by extension, in salsa are built around a two-bar rhythmic pattern called the *clave*. Playing *en clave* is essential for the music to "sound right" and for the dancers to stay in step with it (ex. 5). Second, the "melody" instruments (brass, strings, piano, and bass) are utilized so as to maximize their rhythmic potential. Third, the "rhythm" instruments (all percussion) are played so as to exhaust their melodic capacity. Combined, these factors can create an intelligibility problem for many U.S. listeners.

Appreciating salsa music in the United States takes more than including an excluded culture; we must rethink musical concepts as well as the culture of listening. Just as the Latin alphabet cannot convey the sounds required to speak Japanese, Chinese, Yoruba, and other non-Western languages, the concepts of "rhythm" and "melody" as commonly understood within the Western art music tradition cannot adequately represent what Afro-Latino musicians play or what their audiences might hear. The Western concept of "rhythm," for example, leads to a tendency of ignoring the melodic aspects of drumming.

SALSA AND ETHNIC IDENTITY

Studies of salsa in the United States often focus on its use as a vehicle for ethnic identity. Professor Frances Aparicio makes the argument explicit: she deals with salsa not as a musical genre but as a broader cultural practice and argues that it acts as a form of cultural empowerment. Aparicio regards salsa as a manifestation of a political consciousness through which Latinos are able to reaffirm their cultural identities.[3]

Writings on the music itself have argued not only the question of origins but also questions of authenticity and ideology. The struggle over authenticity seems to center on whether musicians who do not research the roots in traditional, earlier styles of playing should be undervalued. In this perspective, any innovation must be firmly rooted in some basic musical tradition to be authentic. A large proportion of salsa musicians and bands in the United States in the 1970–90 period performed in this "authentic" or, in Cuban, *típico* (traditional) model: they strived to base their arrangements on the study of "original" melodies and rhythms from the 1920s through the 1950s. Perhaps the emphasis on origin and roots in the tension between tradition and creation reflected a hunger for "original" music on the part of large numbers of recent arrivals from the Spanish-speaking Caribbean.

The attempt to provide a Latino pan-ethnic music via salsa has been made in a variety of ways in the United States. First, in some music venues, the audience spontaneously claps the clave beat along with the band. Much should not be made of these exercises because collective acts of this nature are often not really spontaneous, merely participatory, which makes them no less contrived. Second, these efforts cannot succeed when the audience, while being from Latin America, can be nearly as unfamiliar with Spanish-Caribbean music as U.S.-"Anglo" audiences themselves. The clave beat, the rhythmic use of "melody" instruments, and a melodic approach to percussion constitute exotic sounds for many Latin Americans. Perhaps more important have been the valiant attempts at forging pan-Latino sounds that occurred when salsa musicians, led by Willie Colón and Eddie Palmieri, for example, began mixing varieties of rhythms (e.g., Cuban mambo with Puerto Rican *plena* and Brazilian samba) in song arrangements.

The above is not to deny that this genre is playing a role in an ongoing process of identity formation among U.S. Latinos. In New York City, salsa and Dominican merengue are popular among Puerto Rican, Dominican, and Colombian audiences. In places such as San Francisco, Chicago, or Miami, salsa helps provide some Latinos with a shared sense of identity. But the vicissitudes of salsa as a pan-Latino vehicle are manifest in the case of Los Angeles. Although that city boasts a large Latino audience, only a small proportion is interested in Afro-Cuban forms; most Spanish-speaking Angelenos are of Mexican ancestry. While the Caribbean sound—known in Mexico as *música tropical*—and especially the forms *danzón* and mambo have a long tradition in Mexico City, Veracruz, and the states of Yucatán, Tabasco, and Campeche, this is not the case in most of Mexico.[4]

Yet it is important to note the presence of the Afro-Caribbean sound within the Los Angeles Mexican music community. Texas-born, Los

Angeles–raised Poncho Sánchez has maintained the percussion styles of Cuban drummers in Los Angeles jazz and salsa clubs. Many Chicano musicians have successfully played in the Afro-Cuban modes and even combined these forms with rock styles.[5]

Ironically, salsa music may have worked as an antidote to forms perceived as cultural imperialism in the Spanish Caribbean itself. Writer Díaz Ayala points out that in the 1970s and 1980s, the popularity of salsa music helped stem the tide of U.S. rock and acted as a nationalist symbol within the Spanish-speaking Caribbean.[6] On the other hand, the official Cuban government position on salsa was, for many years, more ambivalent. It regarded it as another instance of U.S. imperialism taking advantage of musical sources for purely commercial purposes. This attitude changed in the last decade, with some Cuban musicians themselves judging the popularity of salsa as a positive development because it popularized Cuban music as well.

SALSA CHANGES

In the last two decades, salsa, both in the United States and in Latin America, exhibited a new twist in its development: the appearance of the *salsa sensual,* a romantic ballad with a steady salsa-rhythm background. This new approach represented a shift from Latin American music traditions characterized until then by rather strict separations between "dance music" and romantic "listening" music. As musicologist Deborah Pacini explained at the time, "these categories—romantic and dance music—are more significant in Latin America than in the Anglo-American context. Rock music, for example, is not clearly defined as dance music, nor is it contrasted with a separate category of romantic music. In Latin America, however, these two quite distinct categories form a complementary pair, each fulfilling a different requirement in a musical event, whether it be public or private."[7]

The emphasis on the *salsa sensual* elicited controversy among performers and critics, some of whom saw it as an unfortunate, escapist interlude in the development of the music. To be sure, a male-centered approach characterizes the pleasure principle in the lyrics of many *salsa sensual* songs. But the utilization of the romantic lyrics–ballad format was merely a marketing maneuver designed, in the words of vocalist Andy Montañez, "to bring the youth in." In order to tap into a larger market, one primarily of Latin Americans outside the Caribbean traditions, after 1986, every major salsa group took up *salsa sensual* as part of its repertoire.

To digress for a moment, the discussion over *salsa sensual* brings to the fore issues of representation that can sometimes get lost or confused in translation. Most Afro-Caribbean styles combine dance traditions that originated in Europe and Africa and later evolved into modern "ballroom" dances, such as the Cuban rumba, which was based on a Kongo fertility dance and added Spanish choreographic elements. The body movements of this and other dances have often been represented, especially in Hollywood cinema, as visual imagery suggestive of the "primitive" and as exotic, even "dirty" sexual gratification. Unfortunately, the stereotyping of sensuality as dirty constitutes one of the forces that defines Afro-Latino music in the larger U.S. cultural space.

To return to the issues of commercialism and the lyrics of popular music, we should remember that popular music influences and is influenced by many forces. As author John Storm Roberts has pointed out, while this is not agreeable to a tidy mind, it is often very good for popular music. It is misinformed to regard "commercialism" or "the music industry" as unmitigated evils that affect the "authenticity" of a genre. Much of what is regarded today as "classic" Afro-Cuban music, the "truly authentic," developed in the ambiance of nightclubs and casinos patronized by U.S. tourists in Havana, a testimony to the ability of popular musicians to extract meaning out of sometimes societally demeaning situations.

From a musical point of view, the fundamental change in approach to salsa may have occurred many years earlier, with the introduction of salsa lyrics that carried a political and social message. This message music sometimes privileged text over sound, focused on the story told, and tended to obscure the more characteristic aspects pertaining to melody and rhythm discussed earlier. The popularity of the political salsa of Rubén Blades and others owed much to music producers who perceived the marketability of message songs in Latin America during a period of political effervescence in the 1970s and early 1980s. *Salsa consciente,* as it was called, survived in the United States by being aggressively marketed in Latin America. So, if commercialization is to be blamed for *salsa sensual,* it should be praised for *salsa consciente.*

Expanding the audience by appealing to a wider, more varied range of listeners sometimes requires retreats as well as advances. Performances always demand stylization, which walks a fine line: it always must distort, but only so long as the distortion does not become a caricature. The challenge for practitioners of *salsa sensual* is to make today's distortion tomorrow's authentic tradition. It is too early to tell what the long-term musical impact will be on the genre.

THE SEARCH FOR *SON* AND *SABOR*

The debate among salsa musicians, critics, and audiences about the relative value of *salsa sensual* and the larger presence of salsa as a whole in the American musical soundscape in the 1990s signified in many ways that the genre had achieved maturity and status. For that reason, new developments came under severe scrutiny. But the maturation and establishment of salsa had other important consequences. It produced a vast literature in several languages on the origins and history of salsa. By one estimate, between 1978 and 1994 a total of seventy-three books on salsa were published in Cuba, Colombia, the United States, Spain, Venezuela, Puerto Rico, France, and Belgium. As a result of this outpouring of literature on salsa, a renewed international interest in traditional Cuban music, and in particular in "salsa's principal musical predecessor,"[8] the *son,* began to develop, reaching a veritable boom in the late 1990s. This new development in turn leads to the need to look deeper into the aesthetics of the *son* and Cuban music in general. Within this music the references to physical touch and taste are abundant. The names of tunes ("Sazonando" [Seasoning], "Échale salsita" [Add a Little Sauce], "El rabito del lechón" [The Suckling Pig's Tail]) and the interjections used by musicians (the classic "¡Azúcar!" scream of Celia Cruz) establish a link between sound and *sabor* (both flavor and taste). In the Cuban *son,* musical tones are not tonal colorations but rather flavorful morsels, juices, spices to be felt in one's mouth.

In the next two chapters, I endeavor to investigate the Cuban *son,* its roots, characteristics, and history, and to explore the aesthetic bases of its *sabor.*

CHAPTER TWO

Ontology of the *Son*

The dead go to heaven . . .
the living keep dancing the *son.*
—Miguel Matamoros, "El ciclón"

The beginning of the twenty-first century greets us with a worldwide boom of a Caribbean musical form that first gained international recognition at the beginning of the previous century: the Cuban *son.* The twentieth century witnessed the growth, spread, synthesis, and resynthesis of this popular genre. It provided the foundation for a number of dance trends, such as the 1930s rumba and the 1950s mambo. The *son* became identified with Cuba's nation and nationalism by both Cubans and non-Cubans. It catapulted the island's music to a regionally hegemonic position in the Spanish-Caribbean islands and littoral.

Born in Cuba, the *son* became universal. Like jazz, a native of New Orleans adopted everywhere, the *son* belongs to everyone. Two great musical products of the twentieth century, jazz and the Cuban *son,* would merge in the last half of the century to produce a fun and dynamic hybrid of hybrids that came to be known as Latin jazz. By this time, the *son* itself was already a long way away from its birthplace in eastern Cuba. When first recorded in the 1920s in Havana, it had changed in tempo and feel after mixing with western Cuba's rumba.[1] In the next thirty years, it would influence and merge with other powerful Cuban styles, such as the *danzón* and the bolero. In the last third of the century, the *son* would provide a foundation for a new concept, the salsa movement. In turn, the popularity of salsa led many scholars to research the traditions that came before salsa. Thus, it was the rise of salsa perhaps more than any other musical style that contributed to an increasing awareness among musicians and nonmusicians of the importance and complexity of the early Cuban *son.*[2]

A native of rural Cuba, the *son* became resynthesized and modified in Havana and later in New York, Mexico City, Paris, Los Angeles, and other major international cities where the drums of rumba, mambo, Afro-Cuban jazz, and salsa found receptive listeners, avid dancers, and a nourishing urban ambiance. The instrumental rhythmic format of the midcentury *son* was taken over completely by the modern salsa and Latin jazz ensembles that sport claves, bongos, congas, timbales, cowbells, and *güiros,* the flagship instruments of the *son conjunto* format. Today in large cities all over the world, people dance to the original Cuban *son* and to its friends and relatives the mambo, salsa, and even Latin jazz, a jazz you can still dance to.

It is said that the *son* is a perfect mixture of Spanish- and African-origin musical elements. That simple sentence glosses over a complex story buried in the mysteries of millennia. The musical folklore of Spain is extremely rich and varied. This should come as no surprise, as the Iberian Peninsula has been the home of Celtic and Iberian peoples, Phoenicians, Carthaginians from North Africa, Romans, Visigoths and other Germanic tribes, Arabs, Jews, and Gypsies. In Spain we find many regional musical styles, from the highly rhythmic flamenco guitar genres of Andalusia to the Celtic bagpipe traditions of Galicia and Asturias, the intricate *zortzico* airs of the Basque country, the *jota aragonesa,* and the Catalonian *sardana.* The powerful folklore of the Iberian Peninsula touched many non-Spanish classical musicians who drew inspiration from it: witness the work of Tchaikovsky and Rimsky-Korsakov.[3] Spain developed its own unique variations of European art music, ranging from the sacred, church music approach to the festive *zarzuela* mode. Yet because of its own particular history, Spanish music remained distinct from the strands of European music that developed in the central regions of the continent. One chordophone in particular, while hardly known in the rest of Europe, evolved in Spain, likely from Moorish origin, and became the modern guitar. Spanish artisans and musicians modified early constructions of the instrument and established as well the modern style of guitar playing in the eighteenth century. By the time the *son* arrived officially in Havana from Santiago de Cuba in the early 1900s, four hundred years had passed since the foundation of the first Spanish settlements in eastern Cuba. During this long period, colonists from Andalusia, Catalonia, Galicia, Asturias, the Canary Islands, Extremadura, and other regions of Spain, settled in the area. They brought with them their poetry, songs, dances, and instruments, in particular, the guitar.

During those four centuries, Cuba was also the recipient of the cultural heritage of much of sub-Saharan Africa. Slaves began to arrive in Cuba as early as the first Spanish settlement in the dawn of the sixteenth century. They would continue to arrive until late in the nineteenth century. No other country in the Americas would maintain links to Africa via the slave trade for as long a period as Cuba. As the Spaniards did not themselves engage in the slave trade, the Spanish colonies participated in this nefarious practice by purchasing slaves from those nations that did, namely the Portuguese, French, English, and Dutch. Over the four centuries of the slave trade, the principal nations engaged in it obtained their slaves from varying points and areas of the African continent. African slaves would arrive in Cuba from the entire west coast of Africa below Senegambia, from the interior of the continent, and from its east coast. Although a common Cuban refrain speaks of the Kongo and Carabalí cultural ancestry of the nation, in truth people from nearly three dozen different African linguistic and ethnic groups were forcibly brought to Cuba's shores during the era of the slave trade. The tradition, established by the Spaniards, of allowing African slaves to form fraternal mutual aid societies known as *cabildos,* which were based on a common language, permitted the preservation of certain linguistic, religious, and cultural traditions. Modern research on Africa's ethnic groups has enabled investigators to match the oral traditions of Afro-Cubans regarding their ancestry with specific linguistic and geographic points of origin on the cultural map of Africa. Thus, during Cuba's colonial history, the country became a forced exile for significant populations of Yoruba, Wolof, Fulani, Kissi, Mende, Fon, Ewe, Ashanti, Nupe, Hausa, Ibo, Anga, Bakongo, Songo, Makua, and many other black Africans.[4]

From their various native homes, the deterritorialized Africans, who included innumerable expert musicians and artisans, brought instruments of all types—what ethnomusicologists call idiophones, aerophones, chordophones, and, above all, membranophones. The membranophones, the African drum in its many shapes, forms, and functions, became powerfully present in the Cuban spectrum of musical instruments. A catalog of Cuban drums of African origin would have to include the famed *batá* of the Yoruba, the *yuka* drums of Kongo ancestry, *bembé* drums, the drums of the *tumba francesa, arará* drums, *carabalí* drums such as the *bonkó* and *ekué* of the Abakuá society, the *bokú,* and many more.[5]

The Africans, like the Spaniards, also brought their musical practices. In Cuba, the melodies, songs, dances, and instruments of many parts of Africa converged, and, at the same time, they influenced and were influenced by those brought by the Europeans. This long, rich, and complex process was like an enchanting courtship that led to the powerful and simple description of Cuban music as a marriage between the Spanish guitar and the African drum.

From this pairing comes a wonderful offspring: the *son.* Like its African and Spanish ancestors, the *son* is several things at once: an instrumental music, a popular song, and a people's dance. Instrumentally, the *son* is a collective music requiring a miniature orchestra for its performance, a performance that has been likened to the core of a symphony. As a popular song, the *son* thematizes images of the moment, sometimes as a counternarrative to official history; at their best, the songs evoke pictures of work and leisure, of love and sex. Simple lyrics make a mockery of political misdeeds, speak of love of country, and revel in the dialectics of everyday life. But perhaps above all else, the *son,* like its descendants the mambo, the *pachanga,* the *songo,* and salsa, is something that people listen to with their feet.[6] It is a dance to which people give themselves body and soul, dancing sometimes for hours, tasting the music with their hips—"para bailar bien el son / hay que tener la cintura / dulce como raspadura y caliente como el ron" (To dance the *son* well / you have to have a waist / sweet as crude sugar and hot like rum)—approaching the spiritual levels of trance characteristic of Cuba's sacred ancestry of Arabic and African religious performances.[7] Dancing the *son,* in a manner that Spanish colonial authorities and the Cuban planter aristocracy regarded as immoral and lewd, became a marker of local pride, of *criollismo* and *Cubanismo,* in the late nineteenth and early twentieth centuries.

THE ORCHESTRA

The foundational format of the *son* ensemble consists of a few instruments capable of delivering a deep melodic-rhythmic groove. Central to the ensemble were the claves, a pair of sticks of varying shapes and sizes which, when struck together, produced a pleasant sound that poet Federico García Lorca called a "gota de madera" (wooden raindrop). A couple of polished hardwood sticks would eventually become the clave of choice. *Clavijas* is the Spanish name for the rounded hardwood pegs used in shipbuilding, one of the mainstays of early colonial Cuba. Throughout the colonial period, musicians also engaged in other artisanal work, as carpenters, masons, barbers, and the like. It is likely that as a result of their labor in shipbuilding, they discovered an aesthetic use for the functional wooden *clavijas.* The name *clave* probably derives from *clavija,* and the name of a similar instrument used in the Bahamas—the *cleavers*—is a likely derivative of the Cuban original. While the rhythms beat out on the claves have been traced to African traditional musics, the claves themselves seem to have a definite Cuban origin.

As is the case with many traditional musical instruments, the claves carry gender: the longer, thinner stick is the *macho* (male); the shorter, thicker one is the *hembra* (female). A wide number of rhythmic patterns can be played on this instrumental couple. Like a heartbeat, the claves' beat guides the rest of the instruments and vocalists in the ensemble. In the ancient *son* style known as the *vieja trova* of Santiago de Cuba, the claves play a two-bar phrase known as the *cinquillo,* a pattern with widespread presence elsewhere in the Caribbean, in the Haitian meringue, the Dominican merengue, the Puerto Rican *bomba* (see ex. 1, p. 7 above), the *kwua* and *bele* in Guadeloupe and Martinique, and the Trinidadian calypso. But as the clave rhythm became codified over time, the standard clave beat in the *son* evolved into a five-stroke, two-measure phrase, a "three-two" pattern made up of a strong, syncopated first measure followed by a weaker, metric second measure (see ex. 5, p. 15 above). When this clave pattern is fitted appropriately to an intoned vocal melody or to a line in any melodic instrument, it creates a dynamic tension that strongly implies a dancing resolution.

The vegetal sound of clave-wood raindrops is complemented by the animal-skin tones of the bongos. Many self-reflective *son* lyrics point to the importance of the combination of these two different sounds: "la clave y el bongó / alegran el corazón" declared an early *son* by the Trío Matamoros. "Sin clave y bongó / no hay son" confirmed the Orquesta Aragón in the 1950s.

These two small drums, like the claves, are gendered. The larger membrane, the *hembra,* or female, produces a deeper sound; the smaller head, the *macho,* or male, emits a higher-pitched sound. Like the claves and the *son,* bongos are a transcultural creation. They cannot be found in Africa or Spain; they are a New World invention. Originally only one drum held between the knees provided the accompaniment for the *son* groups. Eventually a second drum, secured with ropes, was hung

Example 6. *Martillo* (bongo)

O=open
S=slap
T=toe
H=heel

S T   T   H   S   T   O   H

outside the knee. Ease of transportation with the increased demand for *son* music led to the modern design, which allows the player to hold both drums between the knees. The accomplished *bongosero* will obtain many tones from these twins: open melodic tones and sharp, closed slaps produced with one, two, three fingers or the full hand. The function of the bongos is dual. The player is expected to provide a firm rhythmic accompaniment, a fairly steady pattern known as the *martillo* (the hammer) (ex. 6).

There are various kinds of *martillo,* depending on the style of the tune; the most commonly known consists of eight separate, distinct tones (eighth notes) that produce a feeling of steady forward propulsion. Accents on the fourth and eighth beats when coupled with the clave beat intensify dancing desires. But the good bongo player is supposed to improvise: the bongos provide tasty fills, unexpected accents, and tonal ornaments. The latter include sliding a finger rapidly and forcefully over the skin of the larger drum head to obtain a humming sound not unlike that of a Brazilian *cuica.* The *bongosero* will engage in "conversation" with the *sonero* (singer) and the melody instruments. *Bongosero* styles vary greatly: some players are smooth, which is excellent for the *bolero-son*; others are so strong that their playing resembles that of a *quinto* soloist in a rumba ensemble. Some are reliable rhythm players, while others are able to mix tones in an ad lib manner that can only be described as lyrical. The very best players possess all these qualities. They are smooth and strong, reliably rhythmic, but at the same time intone a veritable chant as they improvise.

The bongos were the first instrument with an undeniable African past to be accepted in Cuban "society" circles. Thus they became the great equalizers: "Aquí el que más fino sea / responde, si llamo yo," says a poem about the bongos by Cuba poet Nicolás Guillén. International travelers, the bongos left Cuba and were played with unparalleled skill in Afro-Cubop and jazz bands by masters such as Puerto Rico's José Luis Mangual and Italian American Jack Constanzo. In Cuba, the social protagonism and the superb dexterity needed for effective playing made *bongoseros* into legendary musical and folkloric figures. Poets and composers lauded the *bongosero*'s feats. Musicians maintained an oral lore that praises in awe and admiration the accomplishments of the great bongo players: Ramoncito Castro, Armando Peraza, Mongo Santamaría. Some of the greatest were known only by first names or nicknames: Manana, Yeyito, Abuelito, Marino, Ramoncito, El Blanco, Papa Gofio, Papa Kila, Chicho, Hueso, Sinsonte, El Chino, Rolito, and so on. Eventually, bongos became an identity badge for international countercultural youth music, from the Beat Generation to Frank Zappa.

It was Fernando Ortiz's observation that Afro-Cuban orchestras always combined the sounds of wood and skin with that of metal. The *son* orchestra is no exception. To the claves and the bongos we add the *tres* to complete the vegetal-animal-mineral triad. The *tres* is a guitar with three sets of double steel strings. As with the bongos, the origins of the *tres* are lost in the mysterious *montes* (heavily wooded rural areas) of eastern Cuba. We can call it a chordophone conundrum.

As we said earlier, the Spaniards brought the guitar to Cuba. They also carried similar instruments, such as the Arabic *laúd* (oud), which took root in the interior of the island. A culture of guitar playing developed in Santiago de Cuba very early on, which may account partly for the appearance there of both the bolero and the *son*. These styles depend on guitar or guitarlike instruments for their performance. Students of Spanish guitar masters became established in Cuba and passed on new techniques and styles to generations of Cuban guitarists. In the twentieth century, in fact, Cuba has produced two of the world's most prominent guitarists: Leo Brouwer and Manuel Barrueco. (Barrueco hails from the cradle of the *son,* Santiago de Cuba.)

But the Spaniards were not the only source of string instruments or of their playing styles. String instruments of many different shapes and sounds exist throughout the cultures of black Africa, the banjo being the most widely known. Without a doubt, many of those string instruments were transported to Cuba and played there. Although the *son* was and is played with guitars, the instrument of choice became another New World hybrid, the *tres* guitar, or simply, the *tres*. Like a guitar, the *tres* has six strings, but they are organized as three widely separated double-courses of strings. The middle pair of strings is tuned to a unison; the other two are tuned in octaves. What is interesting about the *tres* guitar is that the construction of the instrument limits its harmonic possibilities but nevertheless requires a powerful, percussive strumming motion, which enhances its rhythmic dimension. *Tres* players also favor a strong, percussive picking style. The end result is to privilege a dance aesthetic that points to an African component in the ancestry of this New World artifact.[8]

In the *son,* the role of the *tres* is to accompany the singer at first and then, during a section called the *montuno,* to groove on an ostinato melodic figure based on a few simple chords. This is the section that allows the dancers the greatest freedom to express themselves. These seemingly simple *montunos* pack a musical punch. "How is it possible," asks saxophonist Paquito D'Rivera, "for the montuno, a musical form with such a simple harmonic structure, to be so powerful? It is something electrifying and inevitable; it was meant to be that way."[9] The *treseros,* like the *bongoseros,* have been crucial to the development of the *son,* sometimes as keepers of a tradition, like Compay Segundo (of Buena Vista Social Club fame), and sometimes as fundamental innovators of the genre, like Arsenio Rodríguez.

As the *son* spread and became popular, musicians continued to enrich its thick tonal and rhythmic texture by adding other instruments. To highlight bass sounds, an instrument of well-documented African pedigree, the *marímbula,* was added to *son* ensembles early in the twentieth century. The *marímbula* is usually, and wrongly, defined as a large thumb piano–type box. This description is flawed because, while piano sounds are obtained by striking strings, tonalities of the *marímbula* result from the plucking of metal strips. In fact, the *marímbula* represents the musical predecessor of the later European music box. Known in the Congo River basin region as the *mbira* or *sanza* (or as the *rhumba box* in Jamaica), the *marímbula*'s use throughout Africa and in Cuba for several centuries is well documented. The *marímbula* used in Cuba is normally a large box on which the musician sits. The metal strips are rigid and tuned to a gapped diatonic scale; when plucked, they produce a sound not unlike the quavering resonance of a plucked string of an acoustic upright bass. In the *son,* the *marimbulero* plays the instrument in a dual manner, plucking the metal strips with a downward motion but also striking the wood box for added rhythmic effect when appropriate. In eastern Cuba, musicians in the variant of the *son* known as *changüí* utilize the *marímbula* to this day.

Another local adaptation, the *botija*—an earthen jug with two holes—was used to produce the bass sound in early *son* ensembles. Both the *marímbula* and the *botija* performed the musical function of an upright acoustic bass played pizzicato. Not surprisingly, shortly after the *son* became established in Havana, the acoustic string bass took their place. As with the *marímbula,* the acoustic bass in the *son* plays a prominent rhythmic role and provides the main cues for the movement of the dancers. Some of the great innovators of the *son* in the twentieth century were bass players, notably Ignacio Piñeiro, Israel "Cachao" López, and Juan Formell.

Other instruments also added to the rhythmic density of the *son* sound. More often than not, maracas—handheld rattles or shakers made from gourds and filled with beans, small stones, or seeds—were present in the earliest *son* groups. The voice of the *sonero,* the vocalist in the *son,* rounds out the fundamental format of the *son* ensemble. A good *sonero* has always been hard to come by. The thick, heterogeneous sound laid out by the clave, bongos, bass, *tres,* and maracas requires a vocalist with a thick, bright voice, preferably rough and with a good vibrato. The great *soneros* in history, or *soneros mayores,* had that kind of voice: Miguelito Valdés, Beny Moré, Miguelito Cuní, Roberto Faz, Celia Cruz; as do contemporary *son* vocalists such Rolo Martínez and Cándido Fabré. The *sonero,* as we shall see below, is also expected to improvise, especially during the *montuno.* His improvisations and versification must not only meet certain poetic and melodic requirements but must also remain faithful to the clave and respond to the rhythmic tapestry laid out by the instruments of the *son.*

In the 1920s, *son* ensembles added the trumpet. Melody instruments in the *son* contribute to its dance aesthetic, with an emphasis on rhythmic drive as opposed to harmonic complexity, as exemplified in the sound of the great *son* trumpeters: Lázaro, Chapotín, Florecita, Vivar, Escalante, Armenteros, Varona, Mirabal, and others. With the expansion of the *son* to the *conjunto* format in the 1940s, two instruments were added, the conga drum and the piano. The conga drum, previously used only in rumba and street carnival ensembles, added another, deeper level of sound and altered the role of the *bongosero,* who was now expected to play *martillo* during strophic parts and then switch to cowbell for the *montuno.* Drummers such as Patato Valdés, Armando Peraza, Mongo Santamaría, and Cándido Camero (of later fame as Latin jazz percussionists) became some of the earliest practitioners of the congas in the *conjuntos.* Finally, most *son* ensembles replaced the *tres* with piano or added piano to the *tres.* When transposed to the piano, *montunos* become the basis for piano styles in the modern *son,* contemporary Cuban music, salsa, and, very often, Latin jazz.[10]

THE BIRTH OF THE *SON*

While the details of the recent history and evolution of the *son* are relatively well known, its origins are somewhat obscure. When and where the *son* acquired its distinct characteristics have been the subject of some research and much speculation. A few decades ago, music writers dated the birth of the *son* as far back as the seventeenth century in the eastern province of Cuba called Oriente. Later research brought the date much closer and even suggested the simultaneous appearance of the *son* in different regions of Cuba.[11] Although disagreements persist, the *son* has most often been seen as a product of the uniquely isolated yet multicultural province of Oriente.

Oriente province appears in retrospect as an appropriate site for the development of this powerful form of New World Creole music. Shortly after the initial Spanish settlement in eastern Cuba in the early 1500s, the seat of government and the locus of economic and political power shifted to the new capital in Havana, six hundred miles to the west. The eastern region developed for the next three centuries in a relatively isolated and autonomous manner. A patriarchal form of slavery, with relative ease of manumission, allowed for the early growth of a free black and colored population. Distance from the centers of power permitted widespread activity and itinerant settlement by buccaneers—freelance pirates of the Caribbean—of various nationalities. The plantation system, with its drastic deculturation characteristics, would not appear in the region until well into the nineteenth century.

Oriente witnessed an unusual amount of cultural interchange. Migration back and forth between Oriente province and the islands of Jamaica and Hispaniola contributed to a mixture of various Caribbean cultures at the eastern end of Cuba, northern Jamaica, and western Hispaniola. In Oriente, too, descendants of the original Arawak-speaking Tainos survived in a few locations such as El Caney, Yateras, and Baracoa. The early nineteenth century witnessed a flow into the area of escaping French-speaking plantation owners from Saint-Domingue, who brought their slaves with them when Haiti's revolutionaries declared the first independent republic in Latin America. Later in the century, Chinese laborers were brought to work in the cane fields, as were Jamaicans and Haitians toward the end of the century. While the presence of Hispanic and African elements in the musical culture of Oriente is paramount, the contribution of these various populations is clearly discernible. In the musical nomenclature of the *son* itself we find, for example, not only words of Spanish and African origins but others of Arawak ancestry. Two of the great early *son* performers, Sindo Garay and Lorenzo Hierrezuelo, were descendants of Indo-Cubans. To this day, an oboelike instrument of Chinese origin—the *corneta china*—is played in the street bands of the annual Santiago carnival.

A useful way to approach the possible birth date of the *son* is to examine the date of its arrival and popularization in Havana in the early 1920s. For most of the century, students of the genre have stated over and over that the *son* first arrived in Havana shortly after independence, early in the twentieth century.[12] Presumably, a number of conscript soldiers from Oriente province, drafted into the newly established national army, brought the *son* and its instruments from Santiago de Cuba in the east to Havana in the west. Some evidence suggests that the sounds of the *son* might have already spread throughout the eastern portion of the island. While it is true that there were *soneros* who later became prominent among these young conscripts, other evidence suggests that the movement of the *son* from east to west had begun earlier.

The last two decades of the nineteenth century witnessed great social and economic transformation that affected Cuba's demographics. With the end of slavery in the 1880s and the subsequent modernization of the country's sugar mills, a number of new migratory flows emerged. There was a rapid increase in rural-to-urban migration as former slaves abandoned the countryside for the cities. Intercity migration also took place, while the capital city of Havana especially experienced rapid growth.[13] There was also a slower but steady shift of the rural population from west to east as the center of sugarcane production moved to the provinces of Camagüey and Oriente. These migrations led to greater cultural homogeneity in Cuba and the spread of regional forms throughout the country.[14]

The War of Independence in 1895 caused yet another migration, this time east to west, as the rebel army under the leadership of General Antonio Maceo advanced on the Spanish colonial troops from its base in

Oriente all the way to the westernmost province of Pinar del Río. Oral traditions and other evidence tell of soldiers among Maceo's troops who, in addition to their weapons, carried with them the *tres* and other instruments of the *son* orchestra.[15]

It appears therefore plausible to assert that the *son* had developed in its fundamental form by the second half of the nineteenth century, following a long gestation process. From its birthplace in eastern Cuba, it spread slowly to the rest of the island from the 1880s on, acquiring new traits, certainly slowing in tempo and becoming more strongly rhythmic as it moved west. When the *son* was recorded in Havana in the 1920s, even by groups from Santiago de Cuba, its sound was markedly different from the traditional Santiago sound.

The *son* was born not at a concert but at a dance. The sounds of its instruments and the vocal parts were part of a whole that allowed people to round out the picture with their body movements. Certainly the Creole culture that developed in eastern Cuba in the first three hundred years of colonization originated in populations with ancestral dance traditions: the southern Spanish, the African, and the native Taínos, whose communal *areíto* dances were described by the early Spanish settlers. The Cuban countryside was settled not according to a pattern of villages, as was the case with much of Europe, but in small, dispersed, minuscule settlements, often individual dwellings. The frequent dances, on holidays and during other festivities, brought people together from their distant abodes to commune with others. This is revealed in the nomenclature and language of the *son*. Thus, a form of the *son* in rural eastern Cuba still is called a *changüí,* a word of Bantu origin meaning simply "dance." The lyrics of the *son,* from the earliest known to the most recent orchestrated examples, speak constantly of dancing, perhaps the supreme leitmotif of the genre. Take, for example, the Duo los Compadres in Caimán Aé ("si llegaba un guajiro a *bailar* a un guateque") or in Rita la Caimana ("como *baila* Rita la Caimana"), the Trío Matamoros in El Ciclón ("los muertos van a la gloria y los vivos a *bailar* el son"), in El Paralítico ("bota la muleta y el bastón, y podrás *bailar* el son"), or in Camarones y Mamoncillos ("allá por el año tres se *bailó* mejor el son"), Beny Moré in Son Castellanos ("Castellanos que bueno *baila* usted"), or Bonito y Sabroso ("Que bonito y sabroso *bailan* el mambo"), or Francisco Guayabal ("Que no me hagan más cuentos que en Francisco el elemento sí sabe *bailar* el son"). Generations of Cubans learned that "En Manzanillo se *baila* el son, dando cintura sin compasión," and that even "el bodeguero *bailando* va."

From its very origin, the *son* began to transmute and resurrect in new, resynthesized forms and mixtures, all connected with various dance styles: the *guajira-son,* the *bolero-son,* the *son-cha,* the *danzonete,* the mambo, the *son montuno,* salsa, the *songo,* and so on. From the early nineteenth century onward, the dancing style of Cuban couples became known for its focus on sinuous torso, hip, and shoulder movement, accompanied by the relaxed shuffling of feet. The *son* contributed to the further development of that particular mode of dancing, which became part and parcel of Cuba's artistic and even political identity as it sought independence from Spain.[16]

ANTINOMIES OF THE *SON*

In its mature form, the *son* is divided structurally into two antithetical parts: a closed strophic introduction followed by an open refrain section, or *montuno.* The closed strophic part itself can be seen as the unity of opposites.

The best *soneros* of the twentieth century employed fixed classic Spanish poetic forms such as the four-line *cuarteta* and *redondilla,* called in eastern Cuba *regina,* and the more complex ten-line *décima,* or *espinela,* usually sung in octosyllables.[17] But often they used them merely as a flexible framework for improvisation, sometimes in legendary versification contests, or *controversias.* Beny Moré, Cheo Marquetti, and Joseíto Fernández became justly famous for their ability to utilize the fixed rhymes of the *regina* and *décima* forms as the foundation for freeflowing improvisation.[18] Improvisation on popular themes also meant that colloquial lyrics (often laced with sexual innuendo and double entendre) became intertwined with classic literary forms dating back three hundred years, to Spain's golden age.

The *son*'s movement from the introductory, closed segment to the open *montuno* section shifts the emphasis from melody to rhythm, usually with an increase in the tempo of the tune. In this, the *son* shares a nearly universal characteristic of folkloric dance musics that appear to move from slower to faster tempi as tunes progress. The *montuno* typically involves an antiphonal pattern between the lead *sonero* and a responding *coro* (chorus). Here the repetitive nature of the vocals—which does not exclude limited but noteworthy *sonero* improvisation—and the unison character of the *coro* form part of the highly charged rhythmic drive of this segment, which offers opportunities for the instrumentalists and dancers to improvise and compete with each other. The *montuno* segment of the *son* became the basis for Arsenio Rodríguez's *son montuno* of the 1940s, the Pérez Prado mambo, the famed *descarga* sessions of Cachao López, Bebo Valdés, and Julio Gutiérrez in the 1950s as well as Latin jazz jam sessions.

Both poetry and dance depend on rhythm, meter, and tone. Thus, the opposition between the open and closed segments still permits the *son* to remain together in a unity of melody and rhythm, of poetry and dance. The connectedness between poetry and the powerful *son* dancing was perceived by many poets, among whom Nicolás Guillén is the best known. In two collections of poems in the 1930s, Guillén also highlighted other antinomial aspects of the genre: a pleasure orientation grounded in the toil of the Cuban masses in "Quirino con su tres"; the hybrid character of Cuba's ethnic past in "Son no. 6"; and the humble origins of a sophisticated music in "Cógela tu guitarrero."[19] Open versus closed segments, fixed versus flexible poetic forms, repetition versus improvisation, pleasure versus work, black versus white, popular culture versus high art constitute the musical, social, and cultural opposites that mutually attract, and these bonds between opposites cement the *son* as a genre.

Throughout its history, a tension between tradition and innovation—a struggle between another set of opposites—has been the driving force behind the evolution of the *son* genre. Perhaps the most important innovations were those of the blind *tres* player and composer Arsenio Rodríguez. Born in 1911 in Güira de Macurijes, in the province of Matanzas in western Cuba, Arsenio was the descendant of Africans from the Congo River basin in Africa. As a child he learned to speak Kikongo and mastered the instruments and rhythms of his African cultural heritage. An unfortunate accident—he was kicked in the head by a mule—deprived him of his sight at an early age. When he was about four years old his family moved to the town of Güines in the province of La Habana, a town known for its rich Kongo traditions and its intense musical activity.

With the help of relatives and friends, Arsenio mastered the *tres,* the bass, and conga and bongo drums by the time he was a teenager. In the early 1930s, he moved to Havana, where he directed the Sexteto Boston and later became a member of the Septeto Bellamar. His first compositions—*sones* and boleros—date from this period. Arsenio began to make his mark on the *son* in the late 1930s. During this time, a style known as the *afro-son* had become popular. *Afro-sones* put themes about the African and slave past at the center of tunes and incorporated some rhythms from Cuba's African-derived Creole religions into the compositions. Arsenio's composition "Bruca maniguá" differed from other *afro-sones* in its artful and compelling combination of Spanish and Kikongo lyrics and its complex harmonies. Miguelito Valdés, a friend of Arsenio and perhaps the most popular *sonero* vocalist of the period, recorded "Bruca Maniguá," as did, in the United States, the "Latin" orchestra of Xavier Cugat in the early 1940s.

In the 1940s, Arsenio revolutionized the *son* in several ways. As a leader, he expanded the format of the earlier *son* septets by adding a conga drum, a piano, and up to three trumpets, creating what is still known as the *conjunto* format. While other groups had played around with the addition of the conga drum, it was Arsenio who succeeded in

coordinating the sounds of the conga, bongo, cowbell, piano, and bass
to develop a cohesive, driving rhythm in his group. With this format,
the *son* took a major step toward becoming an instrumental music.
Furthermore, in his compositions he developed a new synthesis of the
son by incorporating the inflections and syncopations characteristic of
the ritual music of the Cuban *palo monte* religion of Kongo origin. The
resulting mixture came to be known as *son montuno.* It was played at a
slower tempo than the earlier *son,* and the rhythm instruments—conga,
bass, bongo—were treated less as accompanying elements, allowing
them to speak with their own voices. The slow tempo and absence of a
clearly defined ground beat led some contemporaries to believe that the
new sound would fail among dancers. Mario Bauzá, another innovator
who mixed Cuban music and jazz to create Afro-Cuban jazz, was of
the opinion that, in order to dance Arsenio's music, you had to be
"Cuban, a good dancer, and to make sure, very black!"[20] Yet the *son
montuno* became extremely popular, and throughout the 1940s the Arsenio Rodríguez *conjunto* became one of the most sought-out musical
groups by Havana dancers.

In the late 1940s and early 1950s, Arsenio traveled back and forth between Havana and New York before settling in New York in the mid-
1950s. During these two decades, he wrote a number of tunes, besides
"Bruca Maniguá," that would become standards of Cuban music and
salsa and the basis for Latin jazz jams. Among those we should mention are "El reloj de Pastora," "La yuca de Catalina," "Pa' que gocen,"
"Dundumbanza," "Meta y Guaguancó," "Fuego en el 23" (which became a very popular salsa hit by Puerto Rico's Sonora Ponceña *conjunto*), "Mami me gustó," "Kila, Quike y Chocolate," and "Los Sitios
acere." In the midsixties, Arsenio moved to Los Angeles, where he
passed away in 1970.

Together with Israel "Cachao" López (see chapter 4), Arsenio Rodríguez can be considered one of the most fundamental innovators in
twentieth-century Cuban popular music as a whole. He also had a
tremendous influence on New York and Los Angeles musicians and

helped build the foundations of the salsa movement. At the same time, the complexity of his music attracted jazz-inclined musicians: in the early 1950s, Cuban jazz players led by Bebo Valdés often used Arsenio's tunes as the basis for the Afro-Cuban jazz *descargas*. Into the 1990s, numerous Latin jazz musicians, from Colombia's Justo Almario to Cuba's Chucho Valdés, have reached into the vast reservoir of Arsenio's compositions as a source of inspiration for their improvisations. As musicologist Danilo Lozano has stated, "When you listen closely, certain elements of Rodríguez's compositions are extremely modern—one wonders, 'Was Thelonious Monk listening to Arsenio Rodríguez, or was Rodríguez hearing Monk?' because the music is that rich harmonically."[21]

With the revival of interest in the *son* in the last ten years, many of Arsenio Rodríguez's *son montuno* compositions have been played and recorded by the various ensembles playing Cuban popular music around the world, such as the Buena Vista Social Club, Afro-Cuban All Stars, Ibrahim Ferrer, Cubanismo, and Sierra Maestra.

The century began with the *son* spreading around the world and finished with a revival of the *son*. In this powerful form, a few simple riffs synthesize centuries of history, work, and cultural fusions. Traditional *son* music, like that of the Buena Vista Social Club, speaks to an intergenerational audience. The appeal of the Buena Vista Social Club and other traditional groups is also connected with the fate of salsa. The latter, in great part a descendant of the *son,* had experienced a doldrums period in the early 1990s. Whenever practitioners of salsa or Cuban music are at a loss for ideas or direction, they seem to return to the *son* in its earlier, "pure" form, much as musicians in the United States return to the blues when they run themselves dry.

Today the *son* has become globalized. Its descendants can be found throughout the categories of international popular music awards: in the mambos of Tito Puente and the tropical music of Linda Ronstadt and Gloria Estefan; in traditional salsa as well as the watered-down, pop-oriented, accessible salsa style; and in the jazz improvisations of numerous artists. Today the *son*'s currency is also on the rise in Cuba. In addition to the increased popularity of traditional *son* musicians such as those in the Buena Vista Social Club, Vieja Trova Santiaguera, and Conjunto Sierra Maestra, a singer of traditional *son* and bandleader, Polo Montañez, became one of the most popular performers on the island before his untimely death in late 2002. Since the early 1990s, the island's youth has also enjoyed a new dance synthesis of the *son* with rock-and-roll and funk. This transmutation, first popularized by the musicians of NG La Banda and known as *timba,* demonstrates the continuing vitality of the old *son* form and its ability to reinvent itself for the needs of younger generations who wish to keep dancing the *son.*

CHAPTER THREE

The Aesthetics of *Sabor*

People walk with rhythm, talk with rhythm, . . . eat with rhythm.
—Mario Bauzá, Jazz Oral History Program interview,
Smithsonian Institution

Sin ritmo no hay ná.
—Carlos "Patato" Valdés, in *Sworn to the Drum,*
a documentary by Les Blank

The *son,* and Cuban popular music as a whole, stands out as one of the magical cultural products of the twentieth century. Bebo Valdés might have called them *una rareza del siglo* (an exceptional occurrence).[1] Certainly more than any other cultural form, music has been constructed as a synonym for Cuban national identity by Cubans and non-Cubans alike. Cuban musicians in the twentieth century developed and continue to develop today a unique aesthetic, a *musicalia* not based on fantasies but rather grounded in the quotidian, particular Cuban reality. This aesthetic is built around the concept of *sabor* (roughly translated as "flavor"), the sine qua non of Cuban musicianship: a musician who does not play with *sabor* cannot play Cuban music well. Cuban musicians make constant references to the concept of *sabor.* Two recent examples will suffice: Bebo Valdés entitled his recent CD with Cachao

López, Patato Valdés, and Paquito D'Rivera *El arte del sabor;* bassist Carlos del Puerto in his introduction to the instructional book *The True Cuban Bass* pointedly thanks Cuban bassists for the *sabor* they contributed to Cuban music. As Cuba's writer Fernando Ortiz might say, music has been the island's superior export commodity as well, providing to outsiders more *sabor,* and a different flavor, than contrapuntal sugar and tobacco.

MAKING A LIVING

The story of the development of Cuban popular music in the twentieth century cannot be separated from the day-to-day struggle of many musicians attempting to *resolver* (make do) during hard economic times. Many of those who would reach great success in the 1950s began their careers in amateur radio contests in the 1930s, which they entered looking for the coveted awards: to the winners went a bag of groceries, a cake, or a wristwatch—all prized possessions during a difficult era.

During the 1930s and 1940s, some musicians faced not only the travails of the poor but the obstacles set down by a society where the local racial codes separated people not so much into blood-based "white" and "nonwhite" categories as into perceived "nonblack" and "black" skin pigmentation. Thus, able musicians might record a tune with an orchestra but were prevented from performing in public with the same orchestra because of the blackness of their skin.

Whatever their color, the low pay offered to nearly everyone was such that many talented musicians pragmatically chose other professions in order to survive and played music intermittently or in their spare time. Thus, the example of Mongo Santamaría, an able percussionist who played in the 1930s and 1940s with the Conjunto de Alfredo León, the Lecuona Cuban Boys, the Sonora Matancera, and the Conjunto Segundo de Arsenio Rodríguez as well as with Enrique González Mantici, Bebo Valdés, and others. Yet Mongo had to take a regular job as a mailman; music would not pay the bills. Once he was able to become a full-time musician (in the United States), Mongo would regale his public with some of the best recordings to date of Afro-Cuban religious and folkloric drumming; compose Latin jazz standards such as "Afro-Blue"; and influence U.S. popular music with his particular mixture of Cuban, soul, and jazz styles, exemplified in his version of Herbie Hancock's "Watermelon Man." In Mongo's case, as in that of many others, we see little evidence to fit the stereotype of the spendthrift condemned by a whimsically impecunious character to lead the life of the suffering artist.

The need to pursue employment that would guarantee a basic living explains the life profile of many Cuban musicians, especially those without formal training, who held jobs as construction workers (Ignacio Piñeiro), welders (Ñico Saquito), blacksmiths (Siro Rodríguez), chauffeurs (Miguel Matamoros), longshoremen (Francisco Aguabella), and even prizefighters (Miguelito Valdés and Abelardo Barroso) before succeeding by hard work, dedication, bravado, hustle, and plain luck in establishing a music career. Armando Peraza was a successful boxer and even a star in semipro baseball leagues in the 1930s. He played ball with the famed El Loco Ruiz, whose brother Alberto led the Conjunto Kubavana in the early 1940s. Walking to the ballpark one day with Armando, Alberto Ruiz lamented he did not have a good enough conga drummer to add to his *conjunto*. "Yo mismo toco la conga," volunteered Armando.[2] One of the best Cuban percussionists of all time, Peraza went on to succeed as Kubavana's *bongosero* and contributed to the success of jazzmen George Shearing and Cal Tjader as well as *rockero* Carlos Santana in the United States in subsequent decades.

To complete this socioeconomic sketch, one needs to point out that educated musicians sometimes fared better but often managed only by becoming jacks-of-all-trades: the same individual might, for example, play bass for a *charanga*, cello for the symphony, *violines* for *fiestas de santo*, and live jingles on radio stations in order to survive.

MUSICIANS IN MOTION

It is often said that Cuban music traveled everywhere. While this is true, and very evocative, the music did not travel of its own accord but was carried by traveling musicians. The history of Cuban music can be seen as the history of the territorial displacement of many of the founders and carriers of music traditions. Musicians migrated not necessarily in compliance with an inborn vocation to drift and tramp, but rather in order to negotiate a variety of political, economic, social, family, and personal situations.

As discussed earlier, migrating musicians brought the Haitian *contredanse* and the *cinquillo* to Oriente province in the early nineteenth century. Other migrations of musicians are worthy of note: the back-and-forth migration of *boleristas* between Yucatán and Cuba; the *danzoneros* who spread the *danzón* from Matanzas to La Habana and the *danzonete* all over the island; the *soneros* who traveled from Oriente to Occidente as conscripts of the early-twentieth-century Cuban army; the *rumberos* from Havana who took that form to Santiago; the pianists from Oriente who trekked to Havana when the *conjuntos* of the 1940s decided to add pianos to the old *septeto* ensembles; the Orquesta Aragón, leaving Cienfuegos for the capital.[3]

As musicians traveled and sometimes settled outside of Cuba, they established "bases" of Cuban music outside the island, even "colonized" extensive territories. Consejo Valiente, also known as Acerina, helped established the *danzón* in Veracruz and Mexico City; the Trío Matamoros spread their *son oriental* throughout the Colombian *costa;* Isaac Oviedo visited Puerto Rico and trained the first Puerto Rican *treseros,* and Machito and Machín carried their sound to New York and Spain, respectively. Humberto Cané transplanted the *son* to Mexico City; Julio Cueva took it to Paris; Armando Oréfiche and Don Aspiazu spread Cuban music around the world.

The intimate connection between migratory patterns, social conditions, musical ability, and general showmanship and hustle are exemplified in the lyrics of a well-known *son montuno,* "Alto Songo," by Luis Martínez Griñán (Lilí), as interpreted by Miguelito Cuní:

Yo en Guantánamo nací	Born in Guantánamo
en Santiago fui lechero,	milkman in Santiago
en Placetas carbonero,	charcoal man in Placetas
en Cienfuegos boticario,	pharmacist in Cienfuegos
en Cárdenas funerario,	gravedigger in Cárdenas
en mi Cuba caminante,	in my Cuba a hiker
y ahora que en La Habana estoy	now that I am in Havana
. . . yo me guillo de cantante!	I fake it as a singer
Alto Songo, se quema La Maya	*Alto Songo, La Maya is burning*

MUSICIANS WITH ATTITUDE

That the island's *criollo* (native) mix results from the encounter of Spanish and African elements in Cuba is most manifest in the field of popular music, as indicated earlier. Certainly in no other expressive form of local culture is the African influence more evident. The *criollo* attitude toward music making results in a performativity of a particular sort, in which musicians, in every moment of their construction of a people's *musicalia,* are at the same time performing their *cubanía* (Cubanness). Cuban musicians have preserved, developed, and performed popular genres with utmost seriousness and dedication—belying the notion that musicians are born, not made—but also with a mixture of hustle, showmanship, and ability; they have played their music with a certain kind of rhythm, not in a narrow musical sense, but in the broader generic sense that Mario Bauzá and Patato Valdés allude to in the epigraphs to this chapter and which Antonio Benítez Rojo finds a defining cultural characteristic of Caribbean peoples. I would like to illustrate these claims as concretely as possible.

When it comes to singing, for example, many Cuban vocalists assume a particular approach toward the song. The attitude may be exceptional as in the following cases (to name only a few). "Bola de

Nieve" (Ignacio Villa), singer-*diseur*-plus–performance artist, whose concerts often amounted to mini-docudramas of Cuban social/racial everyday life. Or that of "La Voz del Diablo" (the devil's voice), Beny Moré, whose voice "recorría todo el registro vocal, tonalidades y tempos, se doblaba en frases y gritos, acompañada de pasos bailables, creando una atmósfera envolvente" (ranged the entire vocal register, many tonalities and tempos, grew into shouts and interjections, dancing all the while, creating an irresistible ambiance).[4] Or "La Mujer Diablo la Yiyiyí" (she-devil)—Lupe Victoria Yoli Raymond, also known as "La Lupe," who was variously described as "a musical animal," by Jean-Paul Sartre; the "creator of artistic frenzy," by Ernest Hemingway; and a "phenomenological phenomenon," by Guillermo Cabrera Infante; and whose voice and style have reached cult status among many Latinos and Latinas in New York and Puerto Rico. Or the combined vocal and instrumental sound of Los Van Van, recently described by a North American critic not given to superlatives as "a sound that becomes a palpable force, an almost physical presence that envelops [a] room with irresistible, propulsive rhythms."[5] Or of a number of other contemporary groups, for example, NG La Banda, whose sound has been described by pop music critic Enrique Fernández as "irresistibly funky and impossibly complex." More generally, a particular style among singers is the rule in the case of generations of *soneros, mayores, y menores* throughout Cuba and its musical "colonies," who know the difference between *cantar* and *sonear.*[6]

Classically trained Cuban instrumentalists—who could and did play the symphonies of Beethoven and Berlioz, loved Mozart, Liszt, Brahms, and Debussy—while acknowledging and mastering the European art music tradition, did not sit in awe of its forms and did not feel bound by them; instead, they claimed the freedom to take instruments of European origin for use in popular rhythms, playing in a new, original, and, some might say, wrong way. Ortiz describes *criollo* artists playing the contrabass not only with the bow, but mostly in pizzicato. Unlike the chamber style of the jazzman, these artists played *jalando pa' fuera* so that the strings vibrate louder and strike the surface of the instrument, adding a percussive element and also striking the ribs and back of the instrument with their hands and/or the bow, transculturating the contrabass into a string-percussion hybrid. "The bass in jazz is a refined thing," says Cachao, but "lo de nosotros es candela!" (our stuff is burning hot!).[7]

Other musicians took instruments of African ancestry and developed approaches to obtain new sounds, namely, the drums called *congas,* for which several generations of outstanding *tumbadores* (or *congueros*) honed a technically complex mode of playing. This style, transported around the world, is known in Africa today as the "modern style" of hand drumming. Many of these percussionists were unknown players of *guaguancó, columbia, yambú* (rumba styles); *quinto* (lead conga) players in carnival *comparsas* (street bands) and/or *monibonkó* (sacred drum) masters; some became influential *congueros* in modern dance bands and jazz and Latin jazz ensembles.

Popular instrumentalists in Cuba also developed new artifacts, ingenious *criollo* modifications of the European and African ancestors to play the music they were developing in Cuba. New instruments include the already mentioned melodic *jimaguas* (twins) known as the bongos, the hardwood claves, the *pailas criollas* or *timbales,* now present in the orchestration of everyone from reggae bands to Gipsy pop, and the *tres* guitar. To describe these original creations, composers and arrangers devised an entire vocabulary, musical *cubanismos,* that could describe the unique aspects of the new musical genres where foreign terminologies were found deficient. For example, *moña* defines a section featuring layered, contrapuntal horn lines; *cáscara* refers to the pattern played on the shell or sides of the timbales; and so on.[8]

Finally, these new and old instruments, played with innovative techniques and styles, were successfully molded into special formats. Foremost among these is the *charanga,* which—as Danilo Lozano has argued—constitutes a microcosm of the Cuban culture mix in process.[9] The *charanga,* a unique combination of European-origin instrumentation (violins, flute) and Afro-Cuban percussion, has undergone more than one hundred years of musical evolution.

AQUÍ EL QUE BAILA GANA
(HERE HE WHO DANCES WINS)

The new instruments, performance styles, formats, and attitude, that is, the "rhythm" I am describing, arose in a process of back-and-forth interaction between musicians and dancers/audience. Clearly, making a living required musicians to develop patterns that were crowd-pleasers and got people up to dance. Musicians also devised new styles, responding to the spontaneous dance steps and body movements of ordinary Cuban *bailadores* (dancers), who faced the music with their own similar dose of bravado, showmanship, and ability. Indeed, a dance researcher has concluded recently that "the predominance of torso-initiated movement and undulations in both ordinary Cuban motor behavior and extraordinary dance movements came ultimately from the matrix of dances that emerged as Cuban creole creations, as *cubanía* or Cubanness."[10] Cuban music and dance are inseparable, and musicians, as the saying goes, "tocan al paso que les bailan" (play to match the way people are dancing). Antonio Arcaño spoke often of the influence dancers had on his flute improvisation; Enrique Jorrín has described how he invented the cha-cha-cha by watching how people danced to his earlier *danzones;* Cachao feels that he himself is dancing when playing the bass; "Cuba," said Emilio Grenet, "es un pueblo que baila" (Cubans are a people who dance).[11] "Un compositor," says Adalberto Alvarez, "solo prueba su obra por la reacción del bailador" (The proof of a composer lies in the reaction of the dancers).[12] "In Cuban rap," said a young Cuban rapper, "you have to have more of a dancing rhythm, otherwise here people will not pay attention to you."[13]

Not surprisingly, the majority of Cuban popular music forms, or *ritmos,* correspond to specific dance styles, even the bolero, *una canción que se baila* (a danceable, rhythmic song). This is true of *danzón, dan-*

zonete, guaracha, son, son montuno, mambo, *guaguancó,* cha-cha-cha, *pachanga, guajira, bolero-son, bolero-cha, songo, pilón, conga, mozam-bique, pacá, chaonda* . . . the list is very long, because as veteran Cuban *conguero* Tata Güines says, in Cuba, someone invents a new *ritmo* every day. The great commercial success of some of these *ritmos,* namely, mambo and cha-cha-cha, is due to some extent to the choreographed labor of individual performers, dance couples, and groups who pushed the musician's agendas to the limit. These performers taught others in and out of Cuba how to stage meaning to the new fashions by way of stylish, glamorous, *picante* (saucy), and sexy movements. Outstanding dancers of Cuban music include *rumberas* such as María Antonieta Pons, Ninón Sevilla, and Rosa Carmina; dance couples such as Lilón y Pablito, to whom renowned Cuban singers Miguelito Valdés and Beny Moré paid tribute in their songs; and several formations of the Mulatas de Fuego.

The relation between musician and audience in Cuban music is further enhanced by other *envolvente* (enveloping) aspects of the gen-res. In the *montuno* form, for example, the dancing audience usually becomes further involved by joining the unison *coro* of the tunes. For their part, the *boleristas del filin* mesmerized the listener with the power of their poetic imagery, as in "La gloria eres tú" by José Anto-nio Méndez; deep sentimentality, as in "Oh vida" by Luis Yáñez; and lyrical love of country, as in "Noche criolla" by César Portillo de la Luz. Composers of *sones* and *guarachas* frequently alluded to national everyday events, from the political to the romantic, often in a sly, witty, or picaresque mode, which served to connect the dancer or listener to the vocal performance. Thus the late nineteenth-century *soneros* from Oriente made oblique references to the Spaniards with lines such as "Mamoncillos dónde están los camarones" (the dreaded *voluntarios* that supported the colonial regime dressed in red, thus, *camarones* [shrimps]), "Caimán, aé, dónde está el caimán" (look out for the croc-odile), and "Pájaro lindo voló" (the Spaniards are fleeing). Later song-writers satirized politicians in tunes such as "La Chambelona" and

"Quítate tú pa' ponerme yo." Other authors chose the picaresque double entendre and the tease texts of the *choteo* in the lyrics of "La fruta bomba," "Cuidadito Compay Gallo," "La fiesta no es para feos," "El muerto se fue de rumba," "A romper el coco," and countless other tunes. Still others connected with the audience through the warm glow of recognition of street *pregones,* from "Coco seco" and "Mango mangué" to "The Peanut Vendor."

A steady, lighthearted *desafío,* or jousting stance, tends to color the intensely active relationship between musicians and audience. An example of this face-off is Joseíto Fernández's "Elige tú, que canto yo," a tune in the ancestral Hispanic tradition of *controversias guajiras,* amateur versification contests that are still practiced in the *montes* (rural areas). Foreign performers need to be ready, because Cuban audiences can often strike the same pose. The Hermanas Martí have told the story of how the greatly loved Mexican tenor Pedro Vargas became irritated when singing at a theater in Havana because of repeated whistles from the audience. "Bueno," said he, "si mi arte no gusta aquí, pues me retiro; buenas noches!" (If my art is not appreciated, I will leave; good night!). Back came the response from the gallery: "No te vayas, sí nos gusta . . . pero te chiflamos por gordo" (Don't go, we *do* like you . . . the whistling is because you're so fat).

The musicians' braggadocio tends sometimes toward a tough, *guapo* style, particularly in the case of *rumberos* and *soneros.* "Tú no juegues conmigo . . . que yo como candela," say the lyrics of a *son montuno* by Miguelito Cuní. An artistic *guapería* has been part of the interpretive attributes of some musicians, such as percussionist/*sonero* Rolando LaSerie, whose manner of intoning melodies was called *guapear la canción.* Musicians known during their careers for actual physical toughness were celebrated in song, as in the case of Chocolate Armenteros:

> ¡Um!, ¡um!, ¡um!
> ¡Um!, ¡um!, ¡um!
> Me gusta la guapería . . . [I love being a *guapo*]
> *(Arsenio Rodríguez and Chocolate Armenteros, "Me boté de guaño")*

Let us not forget that musicians who rose from poor and mean circumstances, and for whom music held the promise of social mobility, sometimes brought with them the cultural baggage of the streets. Contemporaries of Chano Pozo have stated that many people thought of Chano more as a street tough (a *guapo*) than as a musician.

To sum up with one last example: the audiences' image of musicians possessed with a special vigor and strength, with *aché,* was not limited to a muscular, masculinist perspective. It extended to women performers as well, as in the case of *bolerista* Olga Guillot, whom poet Jorge Oliva called the *bollipoderosa.*[14]

MUSICAL AESTHETICS AND SOCIAL STATUS

In the popular imaginary, if something comes easy it cannot build virtue; hard work, on the other hand, builds character. The lives and artistic labors of Cuban popular musicians in the twentieth century paint a story of enduring hard work and dedication, both to earn a livelihood and to build a complex musical edifice that "is sensual, of the senses, of physically tasting and touching."[15]

As mentioned in the previous chapter, the titles of Cuban songs are peppered with constant appeals—from "Echale salsita" to "Sazonando"—to the palate, to flavors, to juices, to sauces, a tendency that in a different essay I have called "the gustatory imperative."[16] The humble origins of most popular musicians are implied as well in the metaphoric referencing of ordinary people's foods to suggest the *sabor* of the music being played: "Ñame con manteca"; "Quimbombó que resbala"; "Malanga amarilla"; "Caballeros, coman vianda"; "Arroz con picadillo y yuca"; "Mariquitas"; "Chicharrones"; "Tamalitos"; "Bacalao con pan"; "Guanajo relleno" (all refrains that refer to yams, lard, yucca, rice, and other foods); and so on.

The aesthetic of *sabor* is central to the ability of Cuban musicians to constantly mix formerly separate Cuban genres and to readily incorporate musical elements from other cultures, which are then re-elaborated and flavored to produce newer forms of Cuban music. Thus, from decade to decade, the most characteristically "Cuban" musical expression, whether it was Arcaño y Sus Maravillas, Beny Moré's Banda Gigante, Los Van Van, or NG La Banda, has been in part the result of criollo "versioning" and reinvention. In this way, elements of classical European music, Italian songs, Spanish melodies, blues, jazz, soul, rock-and-roll, Mexican regional music, Colombian regional music, Dominican *bachata,* and rap have been utilized to further develop the national genres. Contemporary Cuban musicians, in and out of Cuba, are constantly reaching into ancestral roots, jazz, and modern music of all kinds as well as into the already rich heritage of Cuban music to fashion new ideas and reflavor old offerings. One need only consider the recent work by Mezcla, Afro-Cuba, Bebo Valdés, Cubanismo, Amadito Valdés, Ernán López-Nussa, Maraca Valle, Omar Sosa, Polo Montañez, Orishas, and many others.

Cuban musicians often produce these results not merely as spontaneous individuals but in conscious and collective ways. The history of Cuban musicians suggests that the evolution of Cuban popular genres is the product of the work of various kinds of music communities that are far from imaginary. There are communities of family members spanning several generations. Some are fairly large and well-known, such as the López family of bass players, which include Cachao, Orestes, their father, Pedro, and sister Coralia, and Orlando "Cachaíto" López; the Valdés family of Vicentico, Marcelino, Alfredo, Alfredo Jr., Oscar, and Oscar Jr.; and the Valdés family of Bebo, Chucho, Mayra, Chuchito, and Leyanis. But there are many other influential musicians that worked in groups of two, three, or four spanning one or more generations.[17]

Cuban musicians have formed focused groups with a conscious goal of developing Cuban musical genres by incorporating technical and instrumental innovations from around the world. One can think of the *filin* community formed around José Antonio Méndez, Luis Yáñez, César Portillo de la Luz, and others; of the continuing tradition of *orquestas de mujeres* (women's bands), beginning with the *charanga* of Irene Laferté and followed by the Anacaonas, Las Trovadoras del Cayo (led by Isolina Carrillo), and others in operation during every decade since then; of the individuals gathered by Bebo Valdés for his *ritmo batanga* experiment, which brought for the first time the *batá* drums into orchestral arrangements; of the musicians (Negro Vivar, Generoso Giménez, Barreto, Tata Güines, etc.) who surrounded Cachao in the 1950s and worked to establish the *descarga* movement; of later collectives of a similar nature such as Los Amigos; of groups well-documented by Leonardo Acosta who took time out to play jazz; of contemporary organizations that labor to preserve the national musical heritage, such as the Casa de la Trova in Santiago de Cuba; and of orchestras that purposefully sought to expand the harmonic palate of rhythm-rich Cuban music by looking at the possibilities offered by jazz, as in the case of the Orquesta Cubana de Música Moderna, the Grupo Afro-Cuba, and Chucho Valdés's Irakere.

The work of individuals and communities over many decades resulted in the development not only of the numerous genres of Cuban music and the various instrumental formats and implied styles but in a unique national school of making music, or *sonear*. For each instrument in contemporary Cuban ensembles, a way of making it *sonar en cubano* was elaborated over many decades by countless musicians.

One would hope, therefore, that the music workers who elaborated and refined Cuban music in the twentieth century might have fared better than their counterparts in the sugarcane or tobacco *vegas* (fields), that the exceptional result of their labors would yield an exalted social and economic position for the musicians, a group that exists near the bottom of the economic ladder in most modern social formations.

Lamentably, the compensation and recognition received by the majority of Cuban professional popular musicians for most of the twentieth century seems inversely related to their contribution to the Cuban *musicalia*. Some of Cuba's most important composers died in misery and largely ignored. That was the case of *trovador* (singer) Manuel

Corona (d. 1950, Havana), who wrote "Aurora," "Mercedes," and "Longina"; of the genial, blind *tresero* Arsenio Rodríguez (d. 1970, Los Angeles), whose enormous contributions to the development of the *son* we described in the previous chapter; and of vocalist Panchito Riset, popular throughout Latin America and Beny Moré's favorite *cantante* (singer), who succumbed in New York to diabetes after having both legs amputated. Others suffered the ostracism of Cuban audiences and were more successful in constructing the Cuban musical heritage in front of foreign audiences. Thus, José Antonio Méndez, one of the leaders of the vocal style known as the *filin* (feeling) movement and the author of such wonderful boleros as "Me faltabas tú" and "Novia mía," spent a good portion of his working career in Mexico City, not Havana.

Still others, probably the majority, received rock-bottom wages for their work. There are many examples of this kind of exploitation, but one should suffice: Anselmo Sacasas, pianist and arranger for the Casino de la Playa dance orchestra, an influential musician whose style inspired Noro Morales and other pianists, called his years with the Casino de la Playa "the most miserable of my life," referring to the minimal remuneration he received.

To the Cuban mass audience for popular music, both on the island and overseas, these examples may not seem unusual or unexpected. This is because of widespread stereotypes with regard to musicians, artists, and performers, which are not particular to Cuban culture. Often a musician's poverty is called a lifestyle and attributed to the individual's own choice. Many musicians, it is said, were "born bohemian." The popular music profession is not regarded as "work." After all, they are merely "playing" music, aren't they? And if it is work, it could not conceivably be hard work, so why should popular musicians expect more generous compensation? Even though popular genres are regarded as music, they appear to some to lack the "seriousness" attributed to other styles of music. The notion of popular musicians as being in this world but not of it extended in Cuba even to some whose work elevated them into that rarefied zone some call serious music. Thus,

Cuban diva Ester Borja, referring to the ostracism accorded by many to Ernesto Lecuona, commented that "la gente ve a los artistas como gente anormal" (people think that artists are abnormal).[18]

These conventional views have been reinforced by modern mass communication, which allows the vast majority of popular music consumers to know performers only through electronic media, recordings, and so forth, lacking the experience of the musicians' performance in live settings. Musicians then become less than flesh-and-blood and acquire whatever characteristics the public wishes to attach to them as part of its cultural imaginary.

NUESTRA MÚSICA ES NUESTRA IDENTIDAD (OUR MUSIC IS OUR IDENTITY)— JESÚS "CHUCHO" VALDÉS

While trying to make ends meet, countless ordinary Cuban musicians, educated and uneducated, contributed invaluably to building a national popular *musicalia,* which includes a corpus of traditions, genres, instruments, technical vocabulary, and instrumental formats and a manner of making that music, or *sonear.* This aesthetic developed not as an abstract product of elite musicians or commercial promoters but in a mass interaction between professional musicians, dancers, and audiences. Because of that, Cuban *musicalia* in turn constitutes one of the most important components of *lo cubano* and is inseparable from its continuing development. This helps explain why Cubans and non-Cubans will more likely react to the tunes of Beny Moré as representative of national culture but not know about the poetry of, say, Regino Boti or the pictorial work of the Grupo de los Once. The cultural performativity of Cuban *musicalia* also supports the often-made observation that Cuban music groups playing in front of live audiences are unique. Something is missing from recordings of the same groups.

Because music unites peoples of different languages and traditions, it has long been a product that transcends geographical borders and cultural frontiers. The current fixation with globalization is nothing new to musicians. As I pointed out at the beginning of this chapter, this is particularly true in the case of Cuban popular music, a most influential and delectable export.

At the same time, Cuba has been exposed throughout the last two centuries to the importation of most forms of music known to humanity; these imports have been welcomed by local musicians, eager to develop their craft and innovate their traditions. It is well known, in addition, that radio and television grew faster in Cuba than in any other country of Latin America and that the development of music during the first two-thirds of this century was driven by the market imperatives of record companies, large and small. The impact of foreign elements, whether commercial or not, via electronic media in a span of more than eighty years has not led to the dilution of the national forms. The *sabor* aesthetic, which thrives in mixing new and old forms, led to Cuban music's growth, enrichment, and increasing popularity: much of the Spanish-speaking Caribbean and vast areas of Latin America and the United States have become musically Cubanized.

Thus I am confident that any news regarding the disappearance of the musical side of Cubanness under the impact of so-called global music and culture—a euphemism for the corporate sound mass-produced in the United States—is greatly exaggerated. The Cuban musicians' aesthetic of *sabor* has been called by Radamés Giro "una fuerza capaz de absorber todo lo que toma en préstamo" (a force capable of digesting everything it borrows).[19] It has done so in the past. All reason and evidence indicate that it will continue to do so in the future.

PART II

On the Road to Latin Jazz

The chapters in the second part of this book review the activities of a number of representative Cuban musicians who, in the period between 1950 and 1980, did much through their artistic activity to consolidate in the United States a musical genre known in its early stages as Afro-Cuban jazz and currently as Latin jazz.[1]

In recent years, public and academic interest in the study of Latin jazz has peaked. Since 1995, a separate Grammy has been awarded for Latin jazz. A proliferation of instructional materials and specialized magazines focus on Latin jazz and salsa. Specialists, if not academics, posit historical questions about the origins and development of the genre. In the following chapters, I argue that Latin jazz as a genre emerged gradually over the past six decades and not, as some would say, "overnight," after the historic meeting between jazz trumpeter Dizzy Gillespie and Afro-Cuban dancer, popular music composer, and drummer Chano Pozo in the late 1940s. To be sure, the histories of Cuban and American music, while parallel and separate, intersected much earlier, as has been clearly shown by several authors in Cuba and the United States.[2]

Musicians from Cuba, Mexico, and other places in the Caribbean were known to be active in New Orleans at the end of the nineteenth century, just as jazz was beginning to emerge. As mentioned earlier, these musicians provided the sound to early jazz that Jelly Roll Morton called the "Spanish tinge." Musical developments in Cuba and the United States during the late 1930s and early 1940s established the precursors to, or the prehistory of, Afro-Cuban jazz. Other writers, including myself, have shown that the fusion of jazz with the Cuban *son* began in the early 1940s in both Cuba and the United States: Leonardo

Acosta and Cristóbal Díaz Ayala have documented the appearance of a homegrown group of jazz musicians in Cuba from the earliest period as well as the familiarity of many Cuban popular musicians with jazz and American music in general. Max Salazar has often recounted the explorations in the fusion of Cuban rhythms with jazz carried out by Mario Bauzá with Machito and his Afro-Cubans in early 1940s New York. Thus, the joint work of Gillespie and Pozo needs to be seen as one large step in a process rather than a totally unexpected break-through.[3]

After the initial enthusiasm for Afro-Cuban jazz, or Cubop, in the United States, the new form received repeated reinforcements, mainly from Cuban *soneros,* which solidified its position in American and Cuban popular music in the 1950s. The second part of this book focuses on the labor of these musicians. The activity of an entire generation of Cuban musicians, in the decades of the 1960s, 1970s, and 1980s, was significant in the expansion of Latin jazz into a separate genre and for the increasing popularity of Cuban rhythms in general.

One should emphasize that many of the fresh infusions that would shape the development of Latin jazz occurred because popular music in Cuba had also undergone important transformations in the 1940–50 period. Thus, while earlier manifestations of the Cuban *son* and rumba associated with bebop-era jazz produced Afro-Cuban jazz, musicians interested in this sound were nourished, as it evolved by the midfifties into what we are calling Latin jazz, by a series of factors: a continuing and simultaneous evolution of the *son* up to the mambo; the modernization of the *charanga* format; new explorations into sacred musics of African ancestry; and the development of the *descarga* movement. These developments began with the innovations introduced by Arsenio Rodríguez (discussed in chapter 2), who changed the *septeto* format of the *son* by adding the conga drum, the piano, and a second trumpet. Rhythmically speaking, Rodríguez's perhaps most important innovation was the successful integration of the deep sound of the conga drum with the activities of the *bongosero,* who was now called for double duty on bongo and *campana*. More or less simultaneously with these innovations, the old *charanga* format was modified with the introduction of the conga drum by the Arcaño orchestra, which, prodded by Orestes and Cachao López, began to play the more *son*-influenced *danzón de nuevo ritmo*.

Two more genres would emerge later in the decade, genres that were no longer just Cuban but truly international in character. The new formulations laid out by Arsenio Rodríguez and the Arcaño-Cachao-Orestes López *troika* laid the groundwork for the success of the Pérez Prado mambo in the late 1940s, which took Cuba, Mexico, the United States, and the world by storm. Much has been written about the mambo. Perhaps one of the most succinct and apt descriptions was provided by a then-obscure young journalist by the name of Gabriel García Márquez, writing for the newspaper *El Heraldo* of Barranquilla, Colombia. The future Nobel Prize recipient in literature called the mambo a "mezcla de rebanadas de trompetas, picadillos de saxofones, salsa de tambores y trocitos de piano bien condimentados" (a mix of trumpet slices, minced saxophones, drum gravy, and diced piano, all well seasoned)—in brief, nothing but *sabor*. The rhythmic complexity and "swing" of the Pérez Prado mambo rekindled the interest of American jazz musicians in exploring Cuban and Caribbean music traditions.

Mambo depended greatly on its popularity as a new and exciting dance form. As mentioned earlier, a number of prominent Cuban women dancers and dance couples must be credited with spreading the appeal of the new dance. Among those that deserve mention are *rumberas* María Antonieta Pons, Ninón Sevilla, Rosa Carmina, the dance group Las Mulatas de Fuego, and the dance couple Lilón y Pablito. It was in the wake of the mambo dance sensation that another important development took place in Cuban music: the invention by violinist Enrique Jorrín of another rhythm for dancing: the cha-cha-cha. The new genre revived the *charanga* format, with its lead flute and violin sound, and brought into prominence the *son*-oriented Orquesta Aragón, which popularized the cha-cha-cha through tunes such as "El bodeguero," "Sabrosona," "Bon-bon chá," "El trago," and many others. Within a few years, the characteristic *sonero* sound of Aragón's veteran flutist Rolando Lozano as well as the key role of dance in the aesthetic of Latin jazz were incorporated by pianist George Shearing into the sound of his quintet.

Two related developments were also important: the end of the 1940s witnessed an upsurge of interest in Cuban musical instruments, melodies, and themes from the vast African heritage of Cuba. Composer and flutist Gilberto Valdés, who worked for a while as the musical director of the dancer Katherine Dunham's troupe in the United States, led this movement. Radio stations featured *guaguancós,* drums, and chants from Santería and other religious traditions and the fusion of Cuban country and Afro-Cuban music developed by Celina and Reutilio. Following in this path, in the early 1950s Bebo Valdés invented the *ritmo batanga,* with a format that, for the first time, incorporated *batá* drums into Cuban popular music—a testimony to the continuing creative vitality of African forms. A related innovation would lead to a refinement of the manner in which Cuban music of all types was played: the development of the *descarga* movement of the 1950s, in which many outstanding musicians participated. This movement shifted the focus to the instrumental, improvisational potential of the music, illustrating the conceptual similarities between jazz and Afro-Cuban styles.

In the 1950s and 1960s, a diaspora of Cuban musicians spread throughout other countries. Many of these musicians had been at the center of the evolution of the Cuban music described above. I have chosen a number of representative individuals (for whom we have extensive oral histories collected in the Smithsonian Jazz and Latino Music Oral History Programs) to illustrate their role in broadening the musical palate of the U.S. listening public and in shaping the history of Latin jazz. These individuals—Cachao López, Mongo Santamaría, Armando Peraza, Patato Valdés, Francisco Aguabella, Cándido Camero,

Chocolate Armenteros, and Celia Cruz—were all, in different ways, important participants in the musical changes in the Cuban scene.

Cachao López has been a player, in both senses of the word, at crucial moments in the development of Cuban music and, later, Latin jazz. Together with his older brother Orestes, he took the initiative in the development of the *danzón de nuevo ritmo,* also known as *danzón mambo,* which reached for the syncopation of the *son* and the deep sound of the conga—a drum previously reserved for carnival or rumba. This combination made the stale *danzón* of the late 1930s more appetizing to dancers. While this modification focused on the needs of a dancing public, Cachao's most famous contribution looked to transform the hottest Cuban rhythm music into a listening style, at least in part. I mean of course the famous Cachao *descargas* of the 1950s. It is true that many people recorded *descargas,* and Cachao was not the first. But his were most influential and are still used as examples of the best jam-session style in Cuban music. In particular, his 1957 "Descargas in Miniature," which featured a roster of outstanding musicians (Richard Egües, Negro Vivar, Rogelio "Yeyito" Iglesias, Tojo Jiménez, Orestes López, Guillermo Barreto, Gustavo Tamayo, and Tata Güines), sought to feature each instrument, both rhythmic and melodic, in the solo mode style. Cachao himself, as he has done throughout his musical career, brought into relief the role of the bass in the ensemble and notably developed the bass *tumbaos* in this recording. His rhythmic approach to the bass helped define the role of the instrument in Latin jazz and influenced the bass in jazz as well.

Few individuals were in a better position to synthesize Cuban musical changes of the 1940s than Mongo Santamaría, who came to the United States in the late 1940s. One of the most commonly told stories about Mongo is that he was a mailman in Cuba before leaving for the United States. This is a fact that Mongo readily admits, for the simple reason that in a country full of unemployed and starving musicians, he was fortunate to keep a steady, paying, government job. This circumstance kept Mongo from establishing himself as a percussionist with any particular group for a long period of time. On the other hand, it allowed him to play and become familiar with an impressive number of the most popular music groups of the 1940s and 1950s. From 1940 on, Mongo played and recorded at one time or another in groups such as Alfredo Boloña, Marcelino Guerra, Alfredo León, the Carabina de Ases, the Sonora Matancera, the *conjunto* of the Hermanos Camacho, the jazz band of the Hermanos Martínez, the Conjunto Matamoros, and the Conjunto Segundo Arsenio as well as in the orchestra at the Mil Diez radio station led by Enrique González Mantici. And there were other groups as well. It is a statement about the quality and abundance of Cuba's rhythm players that a person of the caliber of Mongo was not on the permanent roster of any one group. His career in the United States has been a demonstration of his talent. After his initial recordings with Pérez Prado and Tito Puente, he led the way in the recording of deep-rooted folkloric pieces in the Afro-Cuban tradition; helped developed Latin jazz in the West Coast through his many recordings with Cal Tjader; and pointed Latin jazz to the *charanga* format. What is also interesting about Mongo Santamaría is that he has kept his feet (and hands) firmly planted in the best traditions of *son*- and rumba-based Cuban music while contributing his own personal fusion of R&B, jazz, and Latin sound. His drumming and compositions influenced an entire generation of African American musicians interested in things black, as evidenced by the many recordings by jazz musicians of his tune "Afro-Blue."

Resting, as Latin jazz does, on a solid rhythmic foundation, it is no surprise that four other outstanding percussionists contributed to the growth and continuity of Latin jazz in the United States during this period: Armando Peraza, Patato Valdés, Francisco Aguabella, and Cándido Camero. Peraza was the first of the four to settle in the United States, in 1948, to be exact. While still in Cuba, Armando was one of the first percussionists who played congas for the augmented *conjuntos* when he joined the Conjunto Kubavana in the early 1940s. He also played in the *danzoncte* orchestra of Paulina Alvarez and with Dámaso

Pérez Prado. In the United States, Armando doubled on congas and bongos. He was associated with the highly successful Shearing Quintet, whose *Latin Escapade* LP sold in the tens of thousands in the 1950s, quite a showing for that decade. Peraza also played congas for Pérez Prado in the 1955 hit "Cherry Pink and Apple Blossom White" and, importantly in the history of Latin jazz, for the *Soul Sauce* LP by the Cal Tjader Quintet in the mid-1960s. He "finished" his career with a seventeen-year stint with the Santana Latin rock band. Noted for his superb musicianship, technique, and flashy solos, Peraza led the way to the full acceptance of the bongos and congas into Latin jazz.

What Peraza did for the rhythmic integration of bongos and congas in Latin jazz, Patato Valdés expanded for conga drums. Another of the early *conjunto congueros,* Patato Valdés played for the Sonora Matancera and the Conjunto Kubavana before joining the very popular Conjunto Casino in the late 1940s. He arrived in the United States in 1954, playing at various times with Tito Puente, Machito, and Herbie Mann and recording under his own name a number of important percussion sessions. A master of obtaining melodic tones from his *tumbas,* Patato's name became synonymous with conga drumming through his sponsorship of the Latin Percussion brand, which released several influential instructional LPs. His humor, grace, and showmanship also contributed greatly to the popularity of the conga drum sound in Latin jazz.

Matanzas-born Francisco Aguabella first became known in Havana as one of the *tamboleros* in Jesús Pérez's *juego de batá,* featured at the Sans Souci cabaret in the early 1950s. Recruited by African American dancer Katherine Dunham, Francisco first traveled to Italy for the filming *Mambo,* starring Anthony Quinn and Silvana Mangano. Between 1953 and 1957, he traveled around the world, settling in the United States in 1957. During an amazingly varied career, he has been a percussionist for Frank Sinatra, Peggy Lee, and MALO and has recorded in the Afro-Cuban folkloric mode as well as in Latin jazz and salsa. Aguabella's impact as a teacher is profound and continuing: a master of the *batá,* he has also schooled a growing number of percussionists in the intricacies of religious drumming. Many of his students have themselves become active in the Latin jazz field. Finally, Cándido Camero, who first visited the United States in 1946, brought the Latin coloration of his Afro-Cuban percussion into mainstream jazz in an unparalleled manner. Over a fifty-year career he worked as a sideman and recorded with more than one hundred different jazz and American pop music artists, leaving a profound imprint in the music of the United States.

Afro-Cuban music, and by extension Latin jazz, is extremely rich in rhythm, which places a dance imperative at the center for those who perform it, regardless of the instrument played. Even musicians who play traditional melody instruments, such as trumpet or flute, must articulate *son* and rumba phrasing with the rhythm section. Chocolate Armenteros is a living legend of this tradition, a trumpet player who first played in Havana in the late 1940s with the Arsenio Rodríguez Conjunto. In the 1950s, Chocolate became the first trumpet and musical director of the unique Banda Gigante of Beny Moré. Upon arriving in New York in 1957, Chocolate soon joined the premiere Afro-Cuban jazz band in the United States, the Machito Orchestra. Since then, he has played and recorded with just about everybody in the fields of Latin jazz and salsa and has established himself as the representative of a distinctly *sonero* approach to trumpet playing.

It is widely recognized that Afro-Cuban music is one of the main roots of modern Latin jazz. Celia Cruz was synonymous with the Afro-Cuban sound for fifty-some years. In the 1940s, Celia sang Yoruba chants over Cuba's national radio stations and traveled to Mexico and Venezuela as the singer backing up the mambo dance show of the Mulatas de Fuego. It was her work as the vocalist for the Sonora Matancera in the 1950s that made Cuban dance tunes popular all over Latin America and in the Latino diaspora in the United States. Twenty years later, her collaborations with Tito Puente, Pacheco, Willie Colón, and others led to the diffusion of a pan–Afro-Latino sound via the salsa concept. While not a jazz performer, Celia Cruz has done much to propel the development of Latin jazz musicians and Latin jazz audiences, perhaps because no other individual has so popularized the sounds that lie at the root of Latin jazz.

In conclusion, these individuals represent a handful of a larger diaspora of musicians from Cuba who made important contributions to the development of Latin jazz. Clearly, the decades after Chano Pozo constitute an important period, because it was then that the Latin jazz genre acquired further elements from Cuban popular music and its Afro-Cuban traditions, as well as from the Caribbean and surrounding areas. This period overlaps with the growth and development of the salsa phenomenon. With talent and *sabor,* the Cuban musicians mentioned above, along with many others, were an important part of the development of Latin jazz.

CHAPTER FOUR

Magic Mixture

In early 1995, a CD recording by Israel "Cachao" López received the coveted Grammy Award in the Tropical Latino category. In June of the same year, this Cuban bassist received a National Heritage Fellowship award from the National Endowment for the Arts. Later that month, he was featured at the Playboy Jazz Festival at the Hollywood Bowl in California (fig. 1). The increased visibility of this musician came on the heels of a widely acclaimed documentary about Cachao's musical life, *Como su ritmo no hay dos,* produced by actor Andy Garcia; concerts at the Library of Congress; and appearances at festivals in the United States and Europe.[1]

Yet only a few years before, Cachao's name was virtually unknown, even among most of his fellow Cuban expatriates in the United States. Throughout the eighties he had worked in relative obscurity, playing at weddings and parties in the Hispanic community of south Florida.[2] To a certain extent, it would be appropriate to describe this sudden rise in his relative popularity as based on the kind of passing interest in novelty we have grown to expect from the music business as well as fortuitously astute promotion at a moment of growth for the Latin music market in the United States.[3] But I would argue that the increased audience for Cachao's music went beyond marketing happen-

Figure 1. Israel "Cachao" López. Photograph © Mark Holston.

stance and hunger for ephemeral novelty. Given the close political and economic relations between the North American superpower and its small island neighbor, it is no surprise that the distinct music streams of both countries have often intertwined. Cachao's music is central to the separate yet intersecting histories of the hybrid musics of Cuba and its neighboring countries.

Music of Cuban origins has enjoyed successive peaks of popularity in the U.S. music scene for many years. In the early 1990s, the award-winning recordings of "tropical Latino" music by Linda Ronstadt and Gloria Estefan rode a crest of consumer enthusiasm. In the early 1980s, as described in chapter 1, the salsa boom brought recognition to New York musicians such as Rubén Blades and Celia Cruz, among others. And in the late 1940s, the mambo craze led by Pérez Prado and others left an important imprint on U.S. jazz and popular dance music forms.[4]

Born in Havana in 1918 into a family of musicians, Cachao grew up in the town of Guanabacoa, birthplace of Ernesto Lecuona (composer of "Siboney") and a center of Afro-Cuban music traditions. During a long professional career, Cachao's work has been identified with several genres, such as the *danzón,* the mambo, the salsa complex, and more recently, the revival of a variety of Cuban-origin rhythms. Over the last fifty years, the musical ideas, innovations, and performances of Israel López, "Cachao," have played a significant role in Cuban, and in U.S. pan-Latino, musical development.

FROM THE HABANERA TO THE *DANZÓN*

Of all of the Cuban music genres, the connections between the *danzón* and U.S. music are perhaps the least known. The *danzón,* a couple's dance, derived from the *contredanse*—a figure dance of early-nineteenth-century Europe that inspired classical compositions by Mozart and others. In the hands of expert mid-nineteenth-century Havana musicians—for the most part free blacks and mulattoes—the style acquired a catchy, melodious, rhythmic quality. The variation came to be known as *danza a la habanera,* or simply habanera.[5] It became the preferred dance in the capital of the island's planter society.

The habanera spread rapidly. It was the rage in Spain in the 1850s. Onetime emperor of Mexico Maximilian requested the band play a habanera tune, "La paloma," before his execution by a Mexican firing squad. France's Bizet borrowed freely from a popular habanera for the theme of his *Carmen.* In southern Spain, it developed into the *tanguillo gaditano.* Toward the end of the century, it mixed with the *milonga* in the River Platt region, leading to the development of the Argentine tango.[6]

In the United States, composer and pianist Louis Moreau Gottschalk used the characteristic habanera beat—also called tango beat—in a number of compositions.[7] The habanera became part of the musical tradition in New Orleans, a U.S. city claiming a Caribbean heritage.

Years later, its characteristic syncopation could be heard in early jazz tunes by W. C. Handy and Jelly Roll Morton. The latter was referring specifically to the habanera when stating that all jazz had a particular "Spanish tinge."[8]

In Cuba, the *contradanza* continued to evolve. The incorporation of it into other Afro-Caribbean rhythms led to the *danzón,* a couple's dance that dominated society dancing for several decades.[9] Cachao López and his father, older brother, and sister were important interpreters and innovators of this genre during the first third of the century. Cachao's father, Pedro López, played traditional-style *danzones* and the derivative *danzonetes* with the Neno González Orchestra.[10] His older brother Orestes ("Macho") was a brilliant multi-instrumentalist and innovator. He played piano, cello, and bass, and was one of the first to introduce the trumpet into Cuban popular dance music when he played with the Septeto Apolo in the 1920s. Their sister Coralia was the composer of several popular *danzones,* including the famous "Isora Club."[11]

Prolific composers, Cachao and Orestes would write about three thousand *danzones* for various Cuban orchestras over a twenty-year period.[12] During its heyday, the *danzón* did not make its mark in the United States. Some important *danzoneros* did, however: when the leading *danzón charanga* of Antonio María Romeu came to record in New York in 1927,[13] the band's clarinetist, Mario Bauzá, was so impressed with the jazz scene in that metropolis—then at the height of the cultural explosion known as the Harlem Renaissance—that he returned three years later to stay and join the world of jazz.[14] And Cachao's melody for the *danzón* "Chanchullo," as arranged first by Tito Puente and later by Santana, would become a pop hit in the United States in the 1970s as "Oye cómo va."[15]

THE *SON* AND THE MAMBO

From the early 1920s, the *danzón* bands faced competition in Cuban dance halls from groups of *soneros,*[16] which played the hot dance genre from the eastern part of the island we analyzed in chapter 2: the Afro-Cuban *son*. This new form was eventually brought to the United States, where it led to the "rhumba craze" of the 1930s. (Recall that what were called *rhumbas* in the United States were really Cuban *sones,* not rhumbas.)[17]

As a young journeyman musician, Cachao played all sorts of music. He made his debut with the Havana Philharmonic in 1930. But he had become very interested in the popular *son* styles from an early age. At age eight he had joined a children's *son* group, where he played bongos. Another member of the group, Roberto Faz, would go on to become a leading *sonero* with the Conjunto Casino in the 1940s and 1950s. Later, Cachao continued playing percussion under the leadership of Cuban piano player–*diseur* Ignacio Villa ("Bola de Nieve"), working at movie theaters for silent films.[18] In the 1930s, Cachao would play successively with a number of *danzón charangas*.[19]

He would continue to work closely with leading *son* exponents. In 1935, for example, we find him recording musical radio advertisements with Antonio Machín. And in 1935 and 1936, while playing *danzones* at the Sport Antillano dance academy, he made the acquaintance of Arsenio Rodríguez, then playing *tres* for the Sexteto Bellamar, which alternated playing duties with Cachao's *charanga*.[20] Under the influence of the *son* in the late 1930s, Cachao López, his brother Orestes, and their bandleader Antonio Arcaño put together a number of innovations that completely transformed the *danzón*. On top of freer rhythmic bass *tumbaos* developed by Cachao, the flute carried the melody and improvised over syncopated violin *guajeos*.[21] There were other changes: the *timbalero* added cowbells to his ensemble, and eventually a conga drum was included.[22] These innovations taken together were called the *danzón de nuevo ritmo* (new rhythm *danzón*). They surfaced in various tunes over a period of years, but the one that became legendary was entitled "Mambo" (1938).

The revolution in the *danzón* did not produce an immediate impact. A keen interest in new dances, and in dancing in general, did not characterize the upper-echelon "society" circles of Cuba nearly as much as it did the middle- and working-class societies of color.[23] But about ten years later, one of Cachao's contemporaries, Dámaso Pérez Prado, using different instrumentation and a faster, more intense approach, utilized the earlier innovations to launch a style he named the mambo as an international dance.[24]

The music of Pérez Prado became inmensely popular in Mexico and the United States. In New York, Machito and Mario Bauzá's Afro-Cuban jazz ensemble, Tito Rodríguez's group, and other orchestras provided their own version of the new style, leading to the mambo mania that swept the United States in the early 1950s. As percussionist and ethnomusicologist Anthony Brown has indicated: "The impact of [Cachao's] mambo on American music is as profound as anything developed within the shores of America."[25] The mambo quickly spread worldwide and became an obligatory component in ballroom dancing competitions around the world.

FROM DANCING TO *DESCARGAS*

Cachao continued his professional career as a musician working with popular orchestras as well as the Havana symphony and opera companies. Until 1949, he labored steadily with the Arcaño y Sus Maravillas *charanga* orchestra, one of the stellar dance bands in the highly competitive Havana dancing scene in the 1940s. He also joined fellow musicians visiting from abroad for occasional recording dates or jazz jam sessions. Jazz, of course, had been popular in Cuba from the 1910s onward, perhaps the most popular dance genre of the late 1920s. In 1949, Cachao recorded a number of tropical dance tunes with New York–based pianist Noro Morales.[26] And he became a good friend bassist Milt Hinton, who visited Cuba several times with the Cab Calloway Orchestra in the 1950s and 1960s. Sometimes the two of them would enjoy jamming together with a pianist. Milt Hinton recalls jamming with Cachao to the theme of Sergei Koussevitzky's composition

"Chanson triste," which would become the basis for Cachao's renowned tune "Canta contrabajo."[27]

Cuban musical groups had been traveling through the Caribbean since the late 1930s. The spread of recordings had increased the market demand for Cuban styles. Audiences in Puerto Rico, Venezuela, Colombia, Panama, and other neighboring countries had become familiar with the sound of Trío Matamoros, Isaac Oviedo, Casino de la Playa, and, notably, the Sonora Matancera. It was with Fajardo's *charanga* that Cachao first took his sound outside his native island to the carnivals in Venezuela in 1954 and 1957.[28]

Back in Havana, Cachao played with the Havana Philharmonic, working for several years under the direction of conductor Eric Kleiber as well as distinguished visiting conductors such as Sir Thomas Beecham, Von Karajans, Stravinsky, Heitor Villa-Lobos, and Antal Doraty. He was with the Philharmonic when it presented concerts featuring Heifetz, Rubinstein, and Isaac Stern. With Havana's opera, he worked year after year in the 1940s and 1950s in programs that brought to Havana the likes of Ezio Pinza, Mario del Monaco, and Renata Tebaldi. Cachao also joined show bands supporting visiting Argentine tango singers Libertad Lamarque and Hugo del Carril.

In the 1950s, Cachao made another significant contribution that would affect the development of popular music in his country and have an important effect on styles in surrounding countries, including the United States. Afro-Cuban music provides ample opportunity for long, interesting improvisation, but market constraints had kept recorded tunes to the customary two to three minutes in length. From the early 1950s on, a few Cuban musicians were engaged in improvisational sessions called *descargas* (jam sessions). In 1957, Cachao brought together some of Havana's top musicians and recorded the memorable *Descargas en miniatura* (also called *Cuban Jam Sessions in Miniature*). Although commentators often refer to the 1957 sessions as Cachao's mixture of jazz with Cuban music, there is really no evidence for that conclusion. Cachao himself has stated that he did not have jazz in mind when the sessions were put together.[29] More accurately, one can say that for the first time, the hottest Cuban music was played in a manner designed less for dancing (although it is possible to dance to the tunes) than for listening. Leaving the *danzón* completely behind for this recording, Cachao utilized new bass *tumbaos* based on the *son* and the folkloric Cuban rumbas. Putting the accent on rhythm, he featured solos on congas, bongos, and timbales. Some of the tunes exemplified the role of the five-key flute, the *tres* guitar, and the trumpet in modern Cuban music. The characteristic vocal *coros* of the *son* and the rumba were tastefully added. Cachao played acoustic bass and piano on one of the tunes. The playing styles of instruments in a Cuban ensemble were featured, in a thoughtful and deliberate way, as the titles of the songs indicate: "Trombón criollo," "Estudio en trompeta," "Guajeo de saxos," and so on.

The recording was a veritable clinic on the playing styles of instruments in a Cuban ensemble. It featured outstanding performers on each instrument.[30] Cachao's new *tumbaos* would become de rigueur on subsequent *descargas*. Within weeks, everyone in Havana (and in New York, where musicians followed with interest the Havana styles) was putting together *descarga* recordings. With his 1957 recording and several others that followed it, Cachao led the way in the transformation of Cuban music from primarily a dance form into a more abstract style suitable for listening audiences. Thus Cachao was central to two revolutions in Cuban music: the introduction of elements for a new dance, the mambo, and the transformation of Cuban dance forms to permit a "classical" listening approach.

SALSA

In 1962, Cachao left Cuba and spent the better part of that year and 1963 in Spain. He played in various venues in Madrid and at the Mediterranean resort of Alicante. Coincidentally during this period, he had occasion to play briefly with the visiting Pérez Prado orchestra.[31] In 1963, Cachao settled in New York City. For the next few years, he would play and record with just about every major Latin music group in the city: Tito Rodríguez, Machito, Pacheco, the Fania All-Stars, Charlie Palmieri, and Eddie Palmieri, to name a few. He was with the Tito Rodríguez band in the 1964–66 period when the group was at its peak, arguably the best Cuban-style dance orchestra anywhere at that moment. With Tito, he traveled as far away as Argentina, where they played in Buenos Aires, Rosario, and the Mar del Plata resort.

This was an important period, when Latino youths in the United States, unwilling and unable to identify themselves with the main-stream icons of popular music such as the Beatles, were searching for roots in the realm of Afro-Caribbean sounds. These were, after all, the 1960s, and Cachao was at the right place at the right time. He was one of the musicians that many younger musicians turned to for experience and inspiration. In the late 1960s and early 1970s, musicians in New York acquired the historical and musical knowledge that led to the salsa boom of the late 1970s and early 1980s. Listening to the masters changed and enhanced the younger musicians' knowledge and approach to the music.[32]

Two of Cachao's recordings during his stay in New York became legendary for their influence and impact upon later salsa musicians. The first was part of a group undertaking: the memorable *Tico Descargas Live at the Village Gate* in 1966, which resulted in a triple LP. Cachao played in most of the improvisational tunes and was featured in exciting *mano-a-mano* solos with another great bassist, a long-term fixture in Machito's orchestra, Bobby Rodriguez. The second recording, *Patato y Totico* (1968), featured Cachao on bass, Arsenio Rodríguez on *tres,* and an all-star cast of Cuban percussionists led by Carlos "Patato" Valdés playing various Afro-Cuban drum styles. During this period, Cachao occasionally got together with three other superlative musicians: Tito Puente, Miguelito Valdés, and Charlie Palmieri. The quartet performed a number of miniature *descargas* in various small locales in the New York / New Jersey area. Unfortunately, there are no recordings available of those rare sessions.

New York Latin musicians have long recognized their debt to and admiration for Cachao. In 1976, Puerto Rican music collector and producer René López organized a special concert to honor Cachao at Avery Fisher Hall in New York. Major musicians in the Afro-Cuban tradition participated in an evening of *danzones,* mambos, and *descargas* organized in two segments—much like the concert that actor Andy Garcia would organize more than fifteen years later. Two albums were produced as a result, but with scarce resources for promotion and distribution, this tribute was largely ignored by the Cuban-American community of Miami and other locales.[33]

In the early 1970s, Cachao settled in Las Vegas, where he could count on steady employment and good wages. He played every kind of music imaginable at Caesar's Palace, the MGM, the Sahara, and the Tropicana, and he met and played with legendary bassist Al McKibbon and with Xavier Cugat. During the Las Vegas years, Cachao played baby bass and Fender in addition to his beloved acoustic string bass, and he still took time out to work on another LP for the anthologies *Ekue ritmos cubanos* produced by Louis Bellson and Walfredo de los Reyes. This tour de force of Afro-Cuban percussion featured Francisco Aguabella, Luis Conte, Alex Acuña, Walfredo de los Reyes, Louis Bellson, Cat Anderson, Lew Tabackin, Clare Fischer, Emil Richards, Manolo Badrena, Paquito Hechavarría, Alejandro Vivar, and John B. Williams. For this series, Cachao played both the acoustic bass and electric piano.

Cachao retired in the 1980s to Miami's Cuban community, one with little interest in Afro-Cuban music at that time, except for lip service to singer Celia Cruz. He lived in obscurity for nearly ten years, playing at weddings and family parties, in an occasional jam session, and, for a time, with the local Hansel y Raúl Cuban music band. With Hansel y Raúl, Cachao traveled to Colombia for Cartagena's Caribbean Music

Festival in 1985. He put out a recording of *descargas,* but in general the level of his musical activity dropped to near zero.

But things began to look up in 1989. In that year, Cachao traveled to San Francisco to participate in a percussion fest: the Conga Summit, featuring Daniel Ponce, Patato Valdés, Francisco Aguabella, and others. At this event, longtime fan and actor Andy Garcia contacted Cachao about doing a special concert in Miami. This was the beginning of a new period of renewed activity and, for the first time, broader visibility.

In the next five years, Cachao played and composed tunes for Gloria Estefan's *Mi tierra* as well as Paquito D'Rivera's *Forty Years of Cuban Jam Sessions,* issued in 1993. The Andy Garcia–sponsored concert was a welcome success. In turn, it led to the production of the documentary *Como su ritmo no hay dos;* to tours across the United States and Europe; to the issuing of the award-winning *Master Sessions* in 1994; and to frequent travel to Spain, Mexico, Colombia, England, and France.

MAGIC MIXTURE

In an article about Cachao published in Caracas's leading newspaper, Professor Roberto Hernández of the Universidad Central de Venezuela referred to the musical culture of the Caribbean in this somewhat tongue-in-cheek manner:

> *Lo del Caribe es una cultura superior—no pienso discutirlo y menos con personas de culturas inferiores. Al principio fue el Mediterráneo, el Mare Nostrum, donde confluyeron ubérrimos árabes, asiáticos, celtas, escitas, fenicios, germánicos, godos, helenos, iberos, judíos, ostrogodos, romanos, vándalos, vascos, visigodos. Ahora es el otro Mare Nostrum, el Caribe, con más africanos, y con arauacos, aztecas, caribes, y toda gente del planeta, que se nos adhirió porque esto es mejor, porque ninguna raza es superior, porque todas se están ensamblando en el magma único de la humanidad.*

The Caribbean is a superior culture. I don't intend to argue about it, much less with people from inferior cultures. In the beginning it was the Mediterranean, the Mare Nostrum, where there occurred a most productive influx of Arabs, Asians, Celts, Scythians, Phoenicians, Germans, Goths, Hellenes, Iberians, Jews, Ostrogoths, Romans, Vandals, Basques, Visigoths. Now there is the other Mare Nostrum, the Caribbean, with more Africans, and with Arawaks, Aztecs, Caribs, and all peoples of the planet, who came here because this is better, because no one breed is superior, because all are gathering into the unique magma of humanity.[34]

I would add that through figures such as Israel "Cachao" López, musical culture flowed beyond the Caribbean basin like never before to influence deeply and take root in the United States as well. A humble and highly gifted performer and composer, Cachao has played and recorded with over 240 orchestras and groups in his long professional career, ranging from tango and opera to ballet and jazz. A living encyclopedia of traditional Caribbean forms, he is always open to new waves in popular styles; for example, he loves the rhythmic drive of the Colombian *vallenato,* and he can point to early Cuban performers that anticipated the modern rap styles.[35] Thus, the broad recognition his work has received in the United States, Cuba, Puerto Rico, Colombia, and Venezuela in recent years is well merited.[36]

Cachao's contributions are part of a new movement in musical forms that do not fit comfortably within artificial formulations aimed at an illusory conceptual purity. His music represents a mixture of classical, popular, and folk; of European and African; of dancing and listening. Cachao took an already existing, exciting hybrid—a Cuban musical tradition that had developed its own instruments, nomenclature, and idioms—and stirred in new elements, expanded the tradition's previous scope, and propelled it beyond the Caribbean. If music is, in the words of Cuban poet and patriot José Martí, "the soul of the people," then through the music of Cachao we can hear the souls of people in Cuba, the Caribbean, and the United States.

CHAPTER FIVE

Drumming in Cuban

Mongo Santamaría can be credited with making the Cuban drum known as the conga (or *tumbadora*) into an integral part of U.S. music, whether jazz, rock-and-roll, soul, reggae, or other modern genres. No other percussionist achieved greater impact on the diffusion of Afro-Cuban folkloric music or recognition within mainstream jazz as well as through his own unique mixture of Cuban, jazz, and soul music. Following in the footsteps of Chano Pozo, Mongo's labor, along with that of other percussionists such as Armando Peraza, Patato Valdés, Francisco Aguabella, and Cándido Camero, brought about a transformation in the traditional sound of jazz, rock, and R&B drumming. Today the conga is everywhere, either as lead instrument or as fundamental accompaniment to all kinds of music, from U.S. pop to Mexican *norteña,* from Latin jazz to Las Vegas show orchestras (fig. 2).

The musical biography of Mongo Santamaría reveals a constant back-and-forth between two styles of performance and recording. On the one hand, he distinguished himself as a performer of Cuban music in very traditional forms: folkloric rumbas, mambos, *pachangas,* and so forth. On the other hand, he developed his own style of fusion by combining jazz, Cuban-origin rhythms, and the sounds of soul music. Despite this ambidextrous career, Mongo was, in the end, a Cuban *sonero,*

Figure 2. Mongo Santamaría.
Photograph © Mark Holston.

pure and simple. On several occasions he stated his commitment to maintaining the traditional styles of Cuban music and indeed helped preserve and develop Afro-Cuban drumming styles. His criticisms of salsa, which he considered an imitation of Cuban music, did not make him many friends. Yet he clearly admired and promoted the native sounds of all of the countries of the Caribbean basin.

Ramón "Mongo" Santamaría was born in the Jesús María barrio of Havana on April 17, 1917, the son of Ramón and Felicia. His father worked as a carpenter and mason and participated in the neighborhood activities of a national political party. His mother sold coffee, cigarettes, and candy in a street-corner stand.[1] Mongo scarcely knew his African-born paternal grandfather, who had arrived in Cuba in a contraband slave-trading ship in the second half of the nineteenth century. But his maternal grandmother often cooked for *bembés* of the Santería religion, where Mongo began his drumming apprenticeship.

Growing up in Jesús María, a barrio famous for its drummers and the popular street carnival *comparsa* (band) La Jardinera, he was exposed from an early age to a rich musical environment. The year of Mongo's birth coincided with the year the first Cuban *son* was recorded, the beginning of an era that it is still going strong with the Buena Vista Social Club, Cuarteto Patria, and many other groups.[2] He witnessed firsthand the evolution of the *son* groups, from the original trios and quartets to the expanded *sextetos* and *septetos,* which added a trumpet and substituted the acoustic bass for the folkloric *marímbula.*

Mongo was influenced musically by his maternal uncle, José Rodríguez ("Macho"), who led a neighborhood trio and played maracas with the Conjunto Jiguaní. Mongo's mother wanted her son to learn to play the violin. But after a few lessons, the youngster decided that percussion was his calling. He played maracas and sang with neighborhood groups, La Lira Infantil first and, later, La Lira Juvenil. There were other important sources of inspiration. A cousin on his father's side, Luis Santamaría, was a distinguished *akpwón* (singer) in Lucumí religious events. (He eventually became a founding member of Cuba's national folkloric ensemble.) Mongo decided to take up the bongos after watching the amazing *bongosero* Clemente Piquero ("Chicho")—who later played in Beny Moré's orchestra—perform feats of dexterity on that double-headed Cuban drum.[3]

Mongo was still in his teens when he became a professional musician. He played bongos for a group led by Alfredo Boloña and Marcelino Guerra—the latter the composer of many Cuban and salsa standards such as "Pare cochero" and "Me voy p'al pueblo." Mongo's first gig was at a well-known Havana nightspot, the Eden Concert club. In rapid succession, he went on to play with the most notable *son* groups of the 1930s. He played with the Alfredo León *sexteto* with pianist Silvio

Contreras, composer of the catchy *danzón* "Masacre," and bassist Cristóbal Dobal, who later would join the famed Conjunto Casino of the 1950s. Mongo also played with the Carabina de Ases *sexteto*. He recorded for the first time in the late 1930s with the show orchestra Lecuona Cuban Boys and with the veteran *sonero* vocalist Antonio Machín.

For many aspiring youngsters like Mongo, the dream of becoming a professional musician was nearly impossible given the realities of Cuban social conditions. The musicians' ability to produce music was simply one more commodity in a capitalist market, and as such, it was subject to the tendency toward overproduction characteristic of capitalism. Simply put, there were too many musicians for the jobs available. Cuba's sugarcane monoculture economy, dependent as it was on the United States, translated into structural unemployment in all branches of production. The local economy, built on a weak base, became further dislocated by the severe crisis of the 1930s. Within the vast mass of the unemployed, there was a musical reserve army of musicians desperately seeking opportunities.

Mongo had the good fortune of obtaining, with the help of some of his father's political connections, a well-paying job as a mailman. For eight years, from 1939 to 1947, he did not hold a steady job with any particular orchestra or *conjunto* but rather worked occasionally and for short periods with a large variety of bands, *conjuntos,* and orchestras. Perhaps this situation actually increased Mongo's abilities, allowing him to develop his own unique sound and style as well as the flexibility to play with a wide variety of musical ensembles. His virtuosity was certainly well known: in the early 1940s, he was called upon to record with the Lecuona Cuban Boys and to play live shows at the Mil Diez radio station in Havana and with the Sonora Matancera. The sound of his bongos could be heard on the soundtrack of the 1939 film *Ahora seremos felices.* He recorded with the Conjunto Matamoros, played in the Hermanos Martínez jazz band, and, along with young percussionist Tata Güines, toured with the Conjunto Camacho, which worked as the warm-up band for the Conjunto Casino's shows throughout the island.

In the midforties, the Conjunto de Arsenio Rodríguez was easily one of the preferred groups among serious dancers in Cuba. To satisfy the demands for his repertory, Arsenio decided to organize a substitute *conjunto* that played only his music, calling it the Conjunto Segundo Arsenio. For this group the genial blind *tresero* chose the percussionist Cándido Camero as director and *tres* player and Mongo Santamaría as *bongosero*.

Up until this time, Mongo had played only the bongos in the *son* ensembles. But by the late thirties, the sound of the *son* began to undergo an important transition. Some of the ensembles began to experiment with the deeper sound of the conga drum, which, until then, had been used only in carnival *comparsas* or in street rumbas and religious *bembés*. Mongo cites the famous Conjunto La Llave, led by Rafael "Mañongo" Ortiz, as a pioneer in the use of the conga drum. Other sources point to the Sexteto Afrocubano, directed by *rumbero* Santos Ramírez, as the group that introduced the conga drum to the *son* groups around 1936. Regardless of various recollections, it is indisputable that it was Arsenio Rodríguez, who integrated successfully the sound of the conga drummer with that of the *bongosero*. After Arsenio, the *bongosero* did double duty on bongo and cowbell—a style adopted by all subsequent *son* groups. Likewise, the format of most salsa ensembles—Conjunto Libre, Sonora Ponceña, Oscar de León, Niche, and so forth—follows the pattern of bongo, cowbell, and congas established by Arsenio Rodríguez in the early 1940s.

In the decade of the 1940s, two events of great significance affected the course of Mongo Santamaría's career. The first is the beginning of a long-term association and friendship with *bongosero* Armando Peraza. Armando, as I will discuss in detail in a later chapter, played with Patato Valdés in the Conjunto Kubavana. Armando's origins were extremely humble: before becoming a professional musician, he had earned a living as a street vendor and as a semiprofessional baseball player. In years to come, Mongo and Armando would work together often, and together they would leave a permanent imprint on the percussion styles of younger drummers in Latin jazz. The second event was Mongo's joint work with the influential musician Chano Pozo. Mongo and Pozo already knew each other through their activities in Havana carnival *comparsas* and in popular music in general. But in the mid-1940s, they participated in a joint set of performances with an unusual background.

Earlier in the forties, the noted Coronel Basil Russian ballet company visited Havana for a while. The tour was not very successful, and the troupe finally disintegrated. The company's choreographer, David Lichine, and several of the leading dancers remained in Cuba. Using these dancers and some of the local talent, David Lichine organized a special show, *Congo pantera,* which was featured at one of Havana's preeminent nightspots, the Sans Souci cabaret. The show combined classical elements from Russian choreography with local rhythms and dances in an exotic plot that took place in a mythical African village. Several famous Cuban *rumberos* participated in this production: Vitite, Alambre, and Silvestre Méndez; Mongo Santamaría playing his bongos; and the notorious composer, dancer, drummer, and street-tough Chano Pozo. The result was a mixture of Russian ballet with Afro-Cuban rumba, a magic realist concoction as if imagined by a fiction writer.[4] Only a few years later, Chano Pozo, as a member of the Dizzy Gillespie Orchestra, would open an important chapter in the development of Latin jazz, laying the foundations for the merging of jazz with the most authentic Afro-Cuban rhythms. Mongo Santamaría would soon follow in Chano's footsteps, as would Armando Peraza, Cándido Camero, Patato Valdés, and Francisco Aguabella.

Above all, Mongo Santamaría dreamed of the opportunity to work full-time as a musician. A solid possibility appeared in 1947, when he received a contract to work in Mexico City with the well-known Conjunto Clave de Oro. There was a busy flow of musicians between Mexico City and Havana, both legal and illegal. Some Cuban musicians traveled to

Mexico City to record and stayed. Others would simply get onboard a ship and slip into Mexico at Veracruz without immigration papers.

Mongo decided to work in Mexico, but shortly after arriving he fell ill. He communicated with his old friend Armando Peraza to ask him to come to Mexico to assist him with his contract obligations. The two percussionists worked together in Mexico City for about six months. They had no time to settle down, because they received on short notice an offer to travel to New York City in early 1948. To the Big Apple they trekked, with the stage name of the Diamantes Negros, as part of a show that featured their dexterity on congas and bongos. They also provided the accompaniment to the dance couple Lilón y Pablito, whose rumba dancing prowess was celebrated in song by both Miguelito Valdés and Beny Moré.[5]

Mongo and Armando spent most of 1948 working in New York City. They accompanied Lilón y Pablito, and showed off their drumming ability, at shows at the Teatro Hispano. Mongo worked with Miguelito Valdés at the Apollo Theater in Harlem and at the Palladium with Machito. He also joined a local *conjunto* led by Marcelino Guerra. During that year, Chano Pozo, of course, was the talk of the town, playing congas with Dizzy Gillespie and popularizing his compositions "Manteca," "Tin tin deo," and others.[6] But he would not live long: before the year 1948 was over, Chano Pozo was killed in a Harlem bar in circumstances that remain somewhat nebulous to this day.

New York was an economic mecca for the numerous and hungry Cuban and Puerto Rican musicians that arrived there in the 1940s. Mongo was among those who decided to stay in New York to seek an improved standard of living. But it was easier said than done. First, he had to get his papers in order, something that took him about a year and a half. He returned to Mexico to try to obtain his U.S. entry visa at the Aztec capital, to no avail. While in Mexico, he accompanied the Trío Los Panchos and recorded with the "tropical" orchestra of Arturo Núñez. Back to Havana he traveled, waiting for his immigration status to be resolved, where he continued to ply his trade. He joined pianist

Peruchín Jústiz and trumpet player Chocolate Armenteros in a show starring diva Rita Montaner at the famed Teatro Campoamor; he accompanied the Trío Los Panchos again during one of their periodic visits to the island; and recorded with Puerto Rican *bolerista* Pedro Flórez the tunes "Orgullosa" and "Te doy mil gracias." Finally, he returned to New York City as a permanent resident on October 23, 1950.

He began his new professional life in the United States playing with Johnny Seguí's Los Dandys at the Park Plaza Hotel; shortly after, Mongo began collaborating with the Cuban flutist Gilberto Valdés in the first *charanga* ever formed in the United States. Valdés was the composer of such tunes as "El botellero," "Rumba abierta," and "Yo vengo de Jovellanos." He had stayed in the United States after working as musical director for the Katherine Dunham dance troupe. The Gilberto Valdés *charanga* played regularly at the Tropicana Club in the Bronx. The ensemble included Mongo on timbales, the maestro Alberto Iznaga on violin, Macucho—from the Havana district of Los Sitios—on vocals, and Director Valdés on flute.

Around the same time, "Mambo King" Dámaso Pérez Prado was in New York for a number of recording sessions. Mongo was recruited to play congas—the first time he was ever recorded on conga drums—for the tunes "Lupita" and "Mambo del 65." After these recordings, Mongo joined the Pérez Prado band for a national tour at the height of the "mambo craze," which swept the United States in 1950–51.

During this continental tour, Mongo suffered an accident that almost took his life. The bus that carried the entire entourage—musicians, dancers, instruments, and so forth—veered off the road and struck the steel sidings of a highway bridge in Texas, between Dallas and Houston. One of the band's dancers, Celia Romero, was killed. Mongo was seriously injured, suffering multiple hip and leg fractures. At the local hospital to which he was taken, the physician in charge prepared to saw off his leg rather than attempt to repair the fractures. At that time in Texas, this was common practice when the patient was a black person. Only the opportune, and irate, protest of one of the members of the troupe kept Mongo from losing his leg. This courageous individual, Puerto Rican singer Paquito Sosa, managed to convince the doctor that since Mongo was not "just" an American black but a foreign national, the amputation of his leg might have unforeseen legal consequences. Mongo was in the hospital for two months. This accident had long-term consequences as well. His leg, badly reconstructed, remained crooked for the rest of his life. He had to wear special shoes to support his ankle, and over the years he underwent several hip operations to repair the damage caused by the accident and the poor treatment received at the time.[7]

Literally back on his feet, Mongo rejoined Gilberto Valdés's *charanga* in New York. Shortly thereafter, in 1952, he replaced Frankie Colón as the *tumbador* for the Tito Puente Orchestra. Puente on timbales, Mongo on congas, and Manny Oquendo on bongo became a formidable rhythm machine for the band. There was no discernable change in quality when Willie Bobo replaced Manny Oquendo sometime later.

With Tito Puente, Mongo Santamaría recorded, between 1952 and 1957, a series of classic LPs, for example, *Cuban Carnival.* This particular album included such tunes as "Pa' los rumberos," "¿Qué será . . . mulata?" and "Guaguancó Margarito." Other important albums recorded in this period were *Puente in Percussion, Puente Goes Jazz,* and *Top Percussion.* The last one included some very complex Afro-Cuban rhythms suggested by another remarkable drummer, Cuban Francisco Aguabella. (See below, chapter 6.)

Besides his work with Puente, Mongo engaged in a wide variety of musical activities during those years. Few people, for example, are aware that it is the sound of his bongos that accompanies the legendary version of Bobby Capó's "Plazos traicioneros," recorded by Vicentico Valdés in New York in 1954. And in 1955, Mongo began to record a series of LPs dedicated in their entirety to Afro-Cuban folkloric music.

The first project was released as a ten-inch LP entitled *Changó*. The recording was a collaboration between Mongo and the notable singer, drummer, dancer, and composer Silvestre Méndez.

A native, like Mongo, of the Jesús María barrio in Havana, Silvestre Méndez was in New York as part of the Mexico-based María Antonieta Pons dance show. While Silvestre Méndez is not widely known except by musicians and musicologists, his compositions were highly successful. He composed "Yiri yiri bon," one of Beny Moré's first successful tunes, and "Te fuiste," a bolero-cha popularized by Panchito Riset. He demonstrated his mastery of Puerto Rican genres, as shown by his tunes "Mi bomba sonó" and "Orizá," which became part of the standard repertoire for Cortijo y Su Combo.

Others who participated in this historic recording included flutist Gilberto Valdés, Patato Valdés, Antar Daly, and Mercedes Valdés. In 1957, after the arrival of Cuban percussionist and *santero* Julito Collazo in New York, four more tunes were added to the originals and the material was re-released on an LP entitled *Drums and Chants*. Also in 1957, Mongo organized, together with Marcelino Guerra and José "Chombo" Silva, a traditional Cuban music group called Orquesta Manhattan. The group was arguably the most swingin' of all New York groups at that time, especially on those occasions when Armando Peraza, during his frequent visits, elected to sit in and play bongos.

In the same year, Mongo traveled to San Francisco and recorded with vibist Cal Tjader the LP *Más Ritmo Caliente*. Its reception was so positive that in 1958, Mongo and Willie Bobo left Tito Puente and moved to San Francisco as part of the newly formed Cal Tjader Quintet. With Tjader, Mongo made a number of recordings that put him at the top of the Latin jazz world. Three of those LPs are worth mentioning, namely *Latino, Tjader Goes Latin,* and *Demasiado caliente*.

During his short years with Cal Tjader, Mongo composed a tune that would become one of the most recorded numbers of the 1960s and 1970s and a standard in the repertoire of all modern jazz musicians: "Afro-Blue." John Coltrane alone recorded "Afro-Blue" half a dozen times, to the point that many in the jazz world think erroneously that Coltrane composed the tune. Others who popularized "Afro-Blue" include drummer Max Roach and Oscar Brown Jr.

While with Tjader, Mongo Santamaría recorded exclusively for the Fantasy label. The executives at Fantasy soon realized that it was the attractive and complex sound of Mongo's drums that sold Cal Tjader's music. Soon Mongo was recording for Fantasy under his own name. In 1958 and 1959, he released two new LPs devoted to Afro-Cuban folkloric music, first *Yambú* and then *Mongo.* These two discs represent a clinic on the playing of *guaguancós, columbias, yambús, comparsas,* and other highly rhythmic genres of Cuban music. The musicians in these recordings were a select group of percussionists that included, in addition to Mongo, Francisco Aguabella, Willie Bobo, Armando Peraza, and Carlos Vidal. Additionally, there was a supporting cast that included bassist Al McKibbon, Cal Tjader, and Vince Guaraldi. Among the outstanding moments in these two LPs, one can point to Mongo's bongo solo in "Mazacote," the voice and *quinto* of Armando Peraza in "Chequerequecheque," and the master drumming of Francisco Aguabella in "Macunsere" and "Ayenye."

Impressed by Mongo's success as a leader, the Fantasy label sent him to Havana in early 1960 to produce two more albums under his own name. Mongo and Willie Bobo traveled to Havana, where, in collaboration with local musicians, in particular Niño Rivera, they produced two important recordings. The first focused on *batá* religious drumming and rumbas; the second was devoted to popular dance music forms. The first album, *Mongo in Havana: Bembé,* is a truly authentic folkloric production. Indeed, the liner notes to the LP jacket were written by William Bascom, a distinguished professor of anthropology at the University of California at Berkeley. Bascom was an expert on the Yoruba religion, music, and languages of Nigeria and Cuba.

The scholarly importance and the cultural impact of this album merit a careful look at its contents. Side A is made up of five ritual *toques* on *batá* drums: two for Changó, the Yoruba *orishá* of thunder and drums in Cuba; one for Olla, Changó's wife in the Yoruba pantheon; one for Yemayá, mother of Changó, deity of the waters (syncretized in Cuba with the Catholic Virgin of Regla); and one for Ochún, the *orishá* of love, also identified with the patroness of Cuba, the Virgin of Cobre. The vocal accompaniment included Afro-Cuban singer Merceditas Valdés and Mongo's cousin Luis Santamaría. Mongo himself played the *shékere* for this memorable recording. Side B included five rumbas: three *guaguancós* and two *columbias*. The voices were those of Merceditas Valdés and two other *rumberos*, Macucho and Carlos Embale.

For the second LP, *Our Man in Havana*, the notable *tresero* and composer Niño Rivera did all the arrangements for a group of musicians that included Armando Armenteros on trumpet, Papito Hernández on bass, and a young Paquito Hechavarría on piano in addition to Mongo on conga drums. Two tunes from that recording have stood the test of time, Mongo's "Vengan pollos" and Armando Peraza's "Barandanga."

Upon his return to the United States, Mongo left the Tjader quintet and struck out on his own. He put together a *charanga* with Rolando Lozano—of Orquesta Aragón fame—on flute, Chombo Silva on saxophone, Pupi Legarreta on violin, and Cuco Martínez (a veteran of the Arcaño band) on bass. This *charanga,* named La Sabrosa, released several LPs (*Sabroso, Más sabroso, Arriba la pachanga*). It mixed the sweet sound of the violin and the Cuban flute with harmonies and timbres common to jazz. It was not a great commercial success, but it demonstrated Mongo's ability to put together a group of high-quality musicians to attempt new musical fusions. La Sabrosa only lasted a couple of years, but soon Mongo's experiments would have surprising results.

By 1962, the situation of musicians like Mongo had become economically difficult due to the state of relations between the United States and Cuba. In early 1961, the United States severed diplomatic relations with Havana. This rupture was followed by the U.S-sponsored Bay of Pigs invasion. The missile crisis in the fall of 1962 was perhaps the most dangerous moment of the cold war between the United States and the

Soviet Union. Clearly, the early 1960s were not an opportune moment to market something called "Cuban music" in the United States.

In 1962, Mongo returned to New York and was playing in the various small Latino clubs around the city, barely eking out a living. One day his steady pianist—a young man named Armando (later Chick) Corea—called in sick for rehearsal and sent a substitute, another young jazz pianist named Herbie Hancock. While going through the rehearsal, Herbie mentioned a tune he had just composed, "Watermelon Man." That same night, Mongo's band was playing "Watermelon Man." Within a few months, the tune had gone to the top of the pop music charts in the United States. For the first time—outside of the realm of jazz, with its rather limited audience—the mass listening audience in the United States could hear the distinct sound of a conga drum in a pop tune.

The great success of "Watermelon Man" brought good contracts for Mongo, who became, almost overnight, an important individual in the broad panorama of U.S. popular music. He already had achieved a reputation in the jazz world with "Afro-Blue." Now his capacity to turn a jazz tune into a commercially successful song was proven. For the rest of the decade of the 1960s, Mongo continued to record in the newly invented fusion style characteristic of "Watermelon Man." In a number of relatively successful LPs, he recorded numerous songs borrowed from the soul genre, such as "Cloud Nine," "Cold Sweat," "Green Onions," and "Sitting on the Dock of the Bay."

Mongo's appearance became de rigueur at all the important nightspots in New York, Chicago, San Francisco, and Los Angeles. Year after year, his band played shows at elegant Las Vegas casino hotels. His performances always combined a few tunes in the most traditional Cuban style and others with an orthodox jazz approach, but the majority adhered to his own particular fusion of jazz, soul, and Cuban sounds. When asked about Mongo's band, jazz buffs usually felt it was not a jazz band but something "Latin." Cuban purists lamented that it was not danceable enough. But the fact was that once Mongo's band began to play, the listening audiences—whether lovers of jazz or Cuban music—responded enthusiastically.[8]

Mongo Santamaría's musical career has been called bifurcated. That adjective refers to the two sides of his artistic practice. He maintained—in some recordings—a musical allegiance to the most authentic folkloric sounds of Afro-Cuban music; while in others, he developed a more jazz-tinged approach.[9] Thus, for example, at the same time that Mongo popularized Herbie Hancock's "Watermelon Man," he included in concurrent recordings of the early 1960s the vocals of a Cuban legend: La Lupe.

Lupe Victoria Yolí Raymond, who had been referred to in Cuba as the Mujer Diablo (she-devil), later acquired other nicknames, such as La Yiyiyí, until settling on La Lupe. Her loud, heart-wrenching, sometimes insolent vocals had caused a sensation in Havana in the late 1950s. Writers and artists such as Hemingway, Picasso, and Cabrera Infante flocked to her, and La Lupe became a celebrity among the bohemian Havana crowd.[10] The LP *Mongo Introduces La Lupe* represented La Lupe's debut in the United States. Her career continued with several recordings with Tito Puente. She later popularized tunes by Puerto Rican composer Tite Curet Alonso, in particular "La Tirana" and "Puro teatro."

Mongo's handling of La Lupe exemplifies another aspect of his career, namely, his ability to recognize new talent and provide newcomers with opportunities in popular music and jazz. During the 1960s and 1970s, Mongo's orchestra was a sort of entryway for young artists on their way to becoming well-known composers, bandleaders, and soloists. Besides the cases of Chick Corea and Herbie Hancock, there were others, such as flutist Hubert Laws, Colombian pianist Eddie Martínez, and trumpet player and arranger Marty Sheller.

Throughout the 1970s, Mongo maintained his bifurcated musicalia. His "American" sound remained popular, especially after the addition of Armando Peraza in the early 1970s. With Peraza, Mongo's band stole the show at the 1971 Montreux Jazz Festival in Switzerland with their inspired interpretations of "Watermelon Man," "Cloud Nine," "Come Candela," and others. There was also a soloing duel on congas between Mongo and Armando.

During this period, there was a notable presence of Colombian talent in Mongo's ensemble. Besides pianist Eddie Martínez, Mongo recruited Justo Almario to play flute and saxophone. A native of the Colombian Caribbean coast and the son of a percussionist (Luis "Licho" Almario), Justo was at ease with the entire Caribbean rhythmic panorama. He also had grown up listening to the recordings Mongo made with Tito Puente, Cal Tjader, and others. With Justo Almario as his musical director, Mongo traveled throughout Europe, Japan, and South America. They also presented a series of concerts in Cuba.

With Justo Almario, Mongo returned once again to his Cuban roots in a 1974 LP entitled *Ubané*. In this recording, Mongo used a veteran Cuban *sonero,* Justo Betancourt, on vocals. Mongo dedicated the tune "Manana" to the memory of Agustín Gutiérrez, one of the great bongo and conga players in Cuba in the 1930s and 1940s. Aside from traditional Cuban forms, Mongo and Justo imported a brigade of drummers from Colombia's Caribbean coast to record a Colombian folkloric tune for *Ubané,* the memorable "Cumbia típica."

But the 1970s represented a new era, the epoch of the birth of a new musical condiment known as salsa. Thus, when salsa "chef" Jerry Masucci created the salsa group the Fania All-Stars, he was savvy enough to link Mongo Santamaría to his commercial adventure. Under contract by the Fania All-Stars, Mongo participated in the All-Stars' Yankee Stadium concert, where he went *mano-a-mano* with fellow percussionist Ray Barretto in "Conga bongo."

In the eighties, there were no major changes in the musical directions of Mongo Santamaría. He joined Dizzy Gillespie as one of the participants in the Montreux Jazz Festival of 1981. Gillespie and Mongo got together for a performance of Gershwin's "Summertime" for that occasion. In 1984, Mongo released an LP with abundant motifs and themes from the Anglophone Caribbean. *Soca Me Nice* was an important recording for other reasons as well. In it, Mongo introduced another talented percussionist, Humberto "Nengue" Hernández. And Mongo's longtime arranger, Marty Sheller, anticipated, by more than twelve years, salsa versions of the Beatles with his interesting version of the Beatles' "Day Tripper."

In the last years of his life, Mongo was afflicted by a series of health problems: two cardiac mishaps plus two hip operations designed to repair the consequences of the bad medical treatment received back in 1950 after the bus accident in Texas. Nevertheless, he continued with his musical activities. Mongo appeared in concerts with new percussion stalwarts, among them his avowed disciple Poncho Sánchez and the marvelous Puerto Rican *conguero* Giovanni "Mañenguito" Hidalgo. In 1996, Mongo released a new CD, *Mongo Returns,* which included pianist Hilton Ruiz. He also appeared in concert with pianist McCoy Tyner.

In 1997, Mongo received a well-deserved tribute at the First International Latin Jazz Festival in Los Angeles, California; present at the celebration for Mongo were his old comrades-in-drums Armando Peraza and Francisco Aguabella; new percussion stars Hidalgo and Marc Quiñones; and several prominent names in Cuban music and Latin jazz such as Cachao, Paquito D'Rivera, and Arturo Sandoval.

When he passed away on February 1, 2003, Mongo Santamaría left behind scores of recordings that run the gamut of modern popular music. He had been an accompanist to a wide range of performers, from Ray Charles to René Touzet; he tutored dozens of disciples, among them the late Willie Bobo and the outstanding Poncho Sánchez. Thanks in great measure to Mongo's historic musical labors, the conga drums ceased to be an exotic musical instrument and became an essential component of modern jazz and its many variants. And despite his fame and success, Mongo Santamaría continued to be an engaging and down-to-earth person. When asked to judge his own musical career, he smiled broadly and stated in a humble manner, "I am a *sonero.*"

CHAPTER SIX

Lords of the *Tambor*

The development of percussion of Afro-Cuban origin in Latin jazz and other U.S. musics such as pop and funk after 1950 depends on the presence of several percussionists in addition to Mongo Santamaría, the subject of the previous chapter. Among nearly a dozen important Cuban drummers, four stand out. Their names are Armando Peraza, Carlos "Patato" Valdés, Francisco Aguabella, and Cándido Camero. As in the case of Mongo Santamaría, each of them possesses very distinct and personal characteristics as a drummer. And they all reached their pinnacle of success and visibility in different ways, in different U.S. cities, and, to a certain extent, in different periods.

PERAZA: MASTER DRUMMER

Two aspects stand out in a review of the musical biography of Armando Peraza. First, during a career that spans five decades, the Cuban percussionist rose to the top of his trade in several significantly different rhythmic genres. A leading conga and bongo drummer for bands with a traditional Cuban sound in 1940s Havana, Peraza went on to excel as the Afro-Cuban percussionist of the George Shearing Quintet in the 1950s and with Cal Tjader in the 1960s. He moved ahead to become an indispensable ingredient in the Latin rock flavor of Carlos Santana of the 1970s and 1980s. Second, all the groups Peraza played with for any length of time (the Conjunto Kubavana, George Shearing, Cal Tjader, and Santana) achieved tremendous success in different epochs, locales, and styles. It is safe to say that this shared success was due in large measure to the presence of Armando Peraza in each of these musical groups. Peraza's career as a master drummer demonstrates not only his technical excellence and musical adaptability but the importance of his "Latin tinge" in American popular music (fig. 3).

Armando Peraza Hernández was born in the La Víbora district of the city of Havana in 1924. Or so his official papers state. But as was the case among poor people in Cuba at that time, his family did not register him as soon as he was born. Thus, the date of his actual birth is a bit of mystery, although he clearly remembers playing in the street as a boy just before the famous 1926 hurricane. It is possible that he was then eight or ten years old, so that his actual date of birth might be sometime between 1914 and 1916. Whatever the case, his childhood was a difficult one: while still an infant he lost both his father and his mother, and he was raised by poor friends and relatives during difficult economic times.[1] From an early age, Armando came into contact with popular expressions of Cuban music: Arsenio Rodríguez rehearsed his *conjunto* in the neighborhood, and Armando became friends with *bolerista* José Antonio Méndez and with the legendary *rumbero* Roberto Torriente.[2]

No one could have predicted that Armando Peraza would become a professional musician. For one thing, hard times required him to make a living as a street vendor of vegetables and fruits as a young teenager. Five days a week he would push a heavy cart from La Víbora to El Vedado and back—a forty-kilometer round-trip—hawking his merchandise. But also, he seemed more interested in sports such as baseball and boxing than in music. Peraza was a good ball player, playing second base and shortstop; he was also a good hitter who usually occupied the second or third spot on the batting line up. He played in semipro leagues, often for the team sponsored by the Ruta 23 bus lines.[3] Some of the other

Figure 3. Armando Peraza *(left)* with author.
Personal collection of the author.

players from those leagues, such as Alejandro Crespo and Avelino
Cañizares, would go on to become stars in the Cuban professional baseball leagues.[4] Yet Peraza had also started playing percussion—first on
wooden boxes, then bongos and congas. He soon became known in his
neighborhood and his reputation began to spread. José Antonio Méndez, who had a program on radio station Mil Diez, invited Peraza to join
his group for a live broadcast. And in 1944, Alberto Ruiz asked Armando to join his Conjunto Kubavana to play congas—or "conga,"
since no one was playing more than one conga except in nightclub
shows.[5] Armando Peraza bought a *tumbadora* for $6 (pesos) and soon be-
came known as a formidable percussionist. When the *conjunto*'s bongo
drummer Cándido Requena left to join the Conjunto Niágara, Armando, who had been impressed with Patato Valdés (at that time working for the Sonora Matancera), convinced Alberto Ruiz to hire Patato to

play congas while Armando would take over the bongo-*campana* duties. Patato and Armando became an immediate hit. A fun-loving pair, sometimes they would warm up for live radio broadcasts by joining in the rehearsals of Havana's top carnival street bands.

The next few years were very busy. Armando played steadily for the Conjunto Kubavana at the Zombie Nightclub, usually every night from 9 P.M. to 4 A.M. The Kubavana Conjunto competed for dancing audiences with the Orquesta Casino de la Playa, the Arsenio Rodríguez Conjunto, Orquesta Melodías del 40, and Arcaño y Sus Maravillas. Weekend dances at La Tropical featured *mano-a-mano* performances between Conjunto Kubavana with Armando Peraza and Sonora Piñón with *bongosero* Yeyito.[6] Sometimes Peraza would be called to replace percussionist Evelio at the Faraón Club show, sit in for Mongo Santamaría at the Los Dandys show at the Sans Souci, take over for Marino with the Conjunto Bolero, or play congas for Paulina Alvarez, "Emperatriz del Danzonete" (Empress of the Danzonette). There were recording sessions with Dámaso Pércz Prado, who was still in Havana, or bongo playing as *quinto* in the shows of famed *rumba columbia* dancer Chamba.

Peraza's first recording, *Rumberito* with Conjunto Kubavana, in which he soloed on bongos, brought him to the attention of everyone in the Havana music business. A major recording, *Rumba en el patio,* would follow. By this time, Armando Peraza had established himself as one of the outstanding bongo players in a city that boasted of the likes of Marino, Yeyito, Cándido Requena, Chocolate Alfonso, Lázaro "Manteca," Mongo Santamaría, Papa Gofio, Abuelito, Yiyo, Marcelo el Blanco, and others. Armando was nicknamed "Mano de Plomo" (Hands of Lead) because of his heavy sound. Famed Havana *conguero* Tata Güines preferred to call him "Mano de Hierro" (Iron Hands).[7] Through these years, Armando played straight-ahead Cuban dance music, often for tourists. There were jazz groups in Havana and some terrific local jazz musicians. But congas and bongos were not yet part of the jazz band format.

In late 1947, Mongo Santamaría asked Armando to come to Mexico City. Travel back and forth between Mexico City and Havana was common for musicians. After all, the two cities were like "sisters when it came to dancing and singing," in the words of Beny Moré's "Bonito y sabroso" tune. Already in the 1930s, the great Ignacio Villa ("Bola de Nieve") had gained fame and prestige in the Aztec capital. Acerina, who settled there permanently, helped develop the very special Mexican *danzón* styles. Mariano Mercerón y Sus Muchachos Pimienta made Mexico City their home base. In the 1940s, a number of other artists had come to the Federal District of Mexico to record and work in the very active nightlife of the city. Miguel Matamoros brought his *conjunto,* which included a young Beny Moré. Dámaso Pérez Prado organized his orchestra and launched his mambo craze from there. Percussionist Silvestre Méndez (author of "Yiri yiri bon") also came and stayed.

Armando arrived in Mexico City to help Mongo, who had fallen ill while performing for the revue *Pablito y Lilón* in the Mexican metropolis. There he joined Mongo in the popular group Clave de Oro.[8] The Mexico City chapter lasted about six months.

In May 1948, Armando Peraza arrived in New York City at the behest of Federico Pagani, manager of the Palladium. Both Armando and Mongo came to the Big Apple with the revue *Los diamantes negros,* which opened soon thereafter at the Teatro Hispano in Harlem, moving later to the Havana Madrid on 49th and Broadway. During his first stay in New York City, Armando lived in a boardinghouse on 135th Street between 7th and 8th Avenues. Aside from playing at the Teatro Hispano and the Havana Madrid, he sometimes sat in with the Machito band at the Palladium. Shortly after his arrival, he participated in a recording of "Tanga" with Mario Bauzá, Charlie Parker, Flip Philips, and Chico O'Farrill as the arranger.[9]

Armando and Mongo soaked in the musical atmosphere of New York City. They watched Chano Pozo entertain audiences at the Apollo Theater. Peraza also played with guitarist Slim Gaillard, who asked him to join his combo. With the four-piece group of Slim Gaillard, Armando toured the United States beginning in late 1948. The group played in Chicago, Kansas City, San Francisco, Baltimore, and the Deep South. Armando fell in love with the City by the Bay, and following some disagreements with Gaillard, he settled in San Francisco in the early 1950s. At the time he resided on Pine Street, near Page. In that period we find Armando Peraza with the group the Afro-Cubans, the house band at the Cable Car Village.

The locale was an artists' hangout. José Ferrer, Ricardo Montalban, Rita Hayworth, and other celebrities could often be seen on the premises. The Afro-Cubans put up a colorful show, complete with fluorescent lights on the congas and even on Armando's playing fingers. The group included the Mexican American Durán brothers (Manuel and Carlos) as well as Bay Area legend *timbalero* Benny Velarde and trumpeter Allan Smith. Vocalists included veteran Sonora Matancera singer Israel del Pino and Juanita Puente. The group traveled up and down California with a repertory that included Mexican as well as Cuban music.

Armando's reputation grew rapidly in the Bay Area and beyond. On occasion he played with African American jazz musicians, such as Art Tatum, in the Fillmore, and he sat in with Miguelito Valdés during the *sonero*'s visits to the Fairmont Hotel. He came in contact with Cal Tjader, with whom he would soon record *Ritmo caliente* for the Fantasy label in 1954.

Bassist Al McKibbon, who had played with Chano Pozo and was touring with George Shearing, persuaded the latter to hire Armando to replace Cándido Camero, who was leaving to form a group of his own. From the early 1950s to the early 1960s, Armando would accompany the George Shearing Quintet during a successful eleven-year period. Armando Peraza was "Shearing's formula for success."[10] Al McKibbon, Emil Richards, and Toot Thielmans rounded out the quintet. The group issued a number of highly successful Latin jazz albums beginning with *Latin Escapade,* then *Latin Lace, Mood Latino,* and *Latin Rendezvous* (the last two featured the great flutist Rolando Lozano), and

Latin Affair. Through these recordings, the jazz and Latin music audiences began to recognize the smooth, almost lyrical feel of Armando Peraza's bongo and conga phrases. The clarity and strength of his sound was heard in other Shearing albums, including *Shearing on Stage, San Francisco Scene, On the Sunny Side of the Strip,* and *George Shearing and the Montgomery Brothers.* Armando Peraza's own compositions can be found throughout the LPs produced during his association with Shearing, such as "Jackie's Mambo," "My New Mambo," and others.

During this period, Armando continued to be sought after for recordings by other bands. He recorded for Mongo Santamaría's albums *Mongo, Our Man in Havana,* and *Sabroso*—all of which included Armando's compositions as well ("Chequerequecheque," "Barandanga," and "Saoco"). He played and/or recorded with Buddy Collette, Pérez Prado, Eartha Kitt, Max Roach, Kenny Clark, Art Blakey, Tony Williams, and Walfredo de los Reyes. He recorded again with Cal Tjader in *Más Ritmo Caliente* (1957) and *In a Latin Bag* (1961). With Shearing, he traveled around the world, playing in Germany, Scandinavia, England, France, and Australia. He also managed a brief visit with his family in Cuba in 1959.

After Mongo Santamaría left the Cal Tjader Quintet to form his own *charanga* group in the early 1960s, Armando joined an ensemble with which he was quite familiar. With Cal Tjader, he toured the United States and Puerto Rico. In 1965, Cal Tjader recorded what would become a classic of Afro-Cuban jazz: the hit album *Soul Sauce,* which included a swinging version of Chano Pozo's "Wachi Waro." For years to come, this tune would become the group's signature as they played in jazz clubs across the United States. Peraza's drums can be heard in every tune on the album, which includes his own "Maramoor." The ensemble sound of Tjader's vibes and Peraza's congas became popular, and it influenced later groups. During Peraza's association with Cal Tjader, the Skye label also produced an album, *Wild Thing,* under Peraza's name.

By the end of the 1960s, Peraza had become an outstanding figure in the city of San Francisco, a member of an informal culture of artists that included Gabor Szabo, the Brazilian guitarist Bola Sete, West Montgomery, and rock bands such as the Jefferson Airplane and the Grateful Dead. In the early 1970s, after several successful years with Cal Tjader, Armando joined Mongo Santamaria's Afro-Cuban jazz ensemble. With Mongo, he traveled to the Montreux Jazz Festival, where they recorded a sensational live performance in 1971. During this time, Armando also performed and recorded occasionally with other artists in a non–Latin jazz mode, including Jerry Garcia, blues stylist John Lee Hooker, and "Queen of Soul" Aretha Franklin. He also played percussion for the soundtrack of the film *Che,* starring Omar Sharif. Before the end of the seventies, he had recorded with Gato Barbieri, Alice Coltrane, and John McLaughlin.

By now, Armando Peraza had succeeded as a percussionist in Afro-Cuban folkloric ensembles playing both congas and bongos (and even *batá* on rare instructional occasions); straight-ahead Afro-Cuban *conjunto* dance music; the Latin jazz of Shearing and Tjader; and the Afro-Cuban jazz of Santamaría and others. But there was more to come. After leaving Santamaría, Armando joined forces for what would be a seventeen-year association with Carlos Santana and his Latin rock sound. The move was not a surprise, since members of Santana's earlier rhythm sections (such as Chepito Areas) had been fans of Peraza in the Bay Area for years. With Santana, Armando would tour the world once again, only this time with a group of much younger rock musicians. He would record a long series of gold albums (*Caravanserai, Lotus, Borboleta, Viva Santana, Amigos,* etc.). For Santana, he would play congas, bongos, and occasionally timbales. Santana would include some of Peraza's compositions too, such as "Gitano" in the 1976 *Amigos.* (In Spain, guitarist Manzanita included "Gitano" on his album *Espíritu sin nombre,* in an arrangement that sounds like an early version of the Gipsy Kings.) Through the late 1970s and the entire decade of the 1980s, Armando Peraza's conga solos brought audiences to their feet at Santana's concerts. Especially when joined by master *timbalero* Orestes Vilató, the sound of Peraza at the lead of the rhythm section of

Santana's band was a guarantee for success in open-air concerts, as in the memorable Cal Jams of the late 1970s in Southern California.

Armando continued to record with other musicians during this period. He can be heard as a guest in one cut of *Batachanga,* an album produced by a number of Cuban-inspired Bay Area musicians including John Santos, Rebecca Mauleon, and Michael Spiro. Forced to retire from the concert circuit in 1991 because of illness, Armando remains active. He has traveled to Europe and Canada to participate in Afro-Cuban percussion clinics. His unique sound can be heard in Linda Ronstadt's Grammy Award–winning CD *Frenesí* and in the soundtrack of *The Mambo Kings.*

Armando Peraza recorded his sound on the skins with highly respected and widely different artists, from the notable Indian percussionist Zakir Hussain to rocker Eric Clapton. One of the most outstanding Cuban percussionists of all time, Peraza was honored at a special Smithsonian Institution event in February 1999. Perhaps the most telling summary of Armando's artistry was a statement by Puerto Rico's José Luis Mangual, who played bongos for New York's Machito orchestra for several decades. Said Mangual: "Peraza is the greatest *bongosero* I've ever heard."[11]

CARLOS VALDÉS: "PATATO" STYLE

The drum known as conga (or *tumbadora*) provided the foundation for modern Cuban dance and *descarga* forms and, later, for most Afro-Cuban jazz music. Indeed, the history of these genres can be read as the history of the famous *congueros:* Carlos Vidal, Chano Pozo, Cándido Camero, Mongo, Patato Valdés, Armando Peraza, Tata Güines, Francisco Aguabella, Papín, and others.

Among all of these percussionists, Carlos "Patato" Valdés stands out as the musician who, almost single-handedly, defined the function of the conga in the Cuban *conjuntos;* expanded its role by using more than one drum in dance ensembles; developed original *tumbaos* to go along

Figure 4. Patato Valdés. Photograph by Enid Farber.

with the larger conga set; and explored to the fullest the melodic and harmonic potential of the conga drums (fig. 4). The jazz public's identification of Patato Valdés with conga drumming in the United States was capped by his endorsement of the first major maker of Afro-Latin percussion instruments, appropriately named Latin Percussion, which included conga drums of the percussionist's own design, the famed "Patato-style" congas.

Carlos Valdés Galán was born on November 4, 1926, the son of Carlos Valdés Cuesta and Juana Galán. Young Carlos grew up in the working-class district of Los Sitios in Havana. The elder Carlos Valdés worked in construction and in a moving agency. His mother, Juana, also earned a living outside the home. She worked in a cleaning business where she mostly ironed clothes. Carlos Jr. completed only the sixth grade and, by all indications, would take up carpentry or work in an auto body shop to earn a living. He received no formal music training.[12]

However, his was a profoundly musical family. Carlos Valdés Sr. had been a member of El Paso Franco, one of the choral *guaguancó* ensembles that emerged in Havana after the turn of the century. In 1916, he organized one of the first *son* groups ever to play in Havana: the Agrupación de Son Los Apaches. Carlos Valdés Sr. played *tres* and *marímbula* for Los Apaches. He is credited with teaching Alfredo Boloña (founder of the seminal Sexteto Boloña) the secrets of the *tres*. According to Patato, two of Carlos Valdés Sr.'s tunes—"Maldita timidez" and "No me desprecies mujer"—would become popular in the 1920s. Los Apaches underwent several permutations until some of the original members formed the famed Sexteto Habanero, the first group to record the *son*. For Carlos Valdés Jr., the conservatory was at home: from his father (and an older brother) he learned to play *tres*, *marímbula*, and maracas. He learned rumba grooves playing on *cajones* (boxes).

From an early age, Carlos Valdés Jr. became familiar with the traditions, chants, and music of Santería (although he would not learn to play *batá* drums until much later). He joined, as his father had done before, a local Abakuá *juego* (Usagaré Mutanga) and learned the intricacies of the *bonkó enchemiyá,* the lead drum of the society's ceremonies. This connection to Santería and the Abakuá provided, together with Valdés's home and the immediate neighborhood of Los Sitios (known for its famous *rumberos*), a rich, if informal, musical culture.[13]

Out of school, Patato Valdés worked delivering milk and bread. As a teenager, he passed the time playing congas for fun in the popular *comparsas* (street bands) of the Havana carnival. He played with Las Boyeras, La Sultana, Los Maharajas, La Leona. He excelled in the lead *quinto* and also became quite a good dancer. He had learned to dance rumba watching his father. But Patato also learned Abakuá dancing, as well as *son* and *danzón*. He tried baseball and boxing. The only instrument that he ever hoped to play professionally was the *tres*. But after listening and watching *tres* players Eliseo Silveira and Niño Rivera, he decided that he was not up to the competition.

Yet all his learning about drums and percussion was about to pay off. The Cuban *sexteto* format of the 1920s had continued to evolve, first by the addition of a trumpet and then, in the late 1930s, by the introduction of the conga drum. Before then, the conga drum was used most commonly in the carnival *comparsas* and in various cabaret shows. Santos Ramírez was one of the first leaders to use the conga drum when, in 1936, he formed his Sexteto Afrocubano—a name later borrowed in New York by Machito and Mario Bauzá for their orchestra.[14] Rafael Ortiz used it in his La Llave group also, according to Mongo Santamaría.[15] As discussed earlier, Arsenio Rodríguez expanded the role and function of the conga in his *conjunto* a few years later, and, simultaneously if not before, the prominent *charanga* Arcaño y Sus Maravillas began to feature the deep sound of the *tumbadora* (as the conga is also known in Cuba). Following the Havana lead, Machito would add conga drums to his New York Afro-Cubans in the mid 1940s.

Patato began to play congas in a *conjunto* led by Remberto Becker in 1943.[16] Later he played for a while in Chano Pozo's Conjunto Azul but found he could not suffer Chano's arbitrary management style. His first major break came in 1946, when he was asked to join a first-class *conjunto* with a twenty-year tradition, the Sonora Matancera. This *conjunto* was to become one of the most enduring representatives of Cuban music in the 1940s and 1950s and was still going strong (outside of Cuba) in the 1990s. Its longevity is attributable to its very distinct sound; for example, when all *conjuntos* in the 1930s were using bongos, the Sonora featured instead the sound of timbales. The group also had a great capacity to constantly refurbish its image by accompanying younger, exciting vocalists. The Sonora's great singer of the 1940s, Bienvenido Granda, would be followed by Puerto Rican star crooner Daniel Santos and later by Celia Cruz. For a while Patato played congas (or rather, conga, for only one was permitted by the bandleader) for the Sonora. He recorded with the group and played music for dance, in particular at the Marte y Belona Dance Academy.

It was at this time that Armando Peraza from the Conjunto Kubavana suggested to Kubavana's leader, Alberto Ruiz, that Patato be brought in as the regular conga drummer so that Armando could concentrate on playing bongos and percussion. Together, Patato and Armando constituted a formidable rhythm machine. The Conjunto Kubavana recorded such collectors' albums as *Rumba en el patio,* recently reissued. The two percussionists also joined forces at the Zombie Club, where they each played up to five congas and other drums in a set-up they baptized the *bongófono.* Patato's fame for both drumming and dancing continued to rise.

The years after 1945 have been called the "age of the *conjuntos.*" The Kubavana competed with other outstanding groups, such as the Conjunto Bolero, the Sonora Piñón, the Conjunto Niágara, the Conjunto de René Alvarez, the Conjunto de Arsenio Rodríguez, and of course the Sonora Matancera. Patato's musical performances brought him to the attention of Miguelito Valdés (no relation), one of the greatest *soneros* in the history of Cuban music. For some years, Miguelito Valdés had worked in the United States, first with Xavier Cugat and later with Machito as well as on his own. As Patato tells the story, Miguelito Valdés sought to persuade Patato to travel with him to the United States, but Patato's father did not allow the trip on account of Patato's young age. So Miguelito Valdés brought a different drummer with him to the United States. And so it was that Patato's "substitute," Chano Pozo, was in New York when Dizzy Gillespie decided to incorporate conga drums into the sound of his bebop orchestra.

Patato stayed in Cuba, where he joined a fast-rising new group, the Conjunto Casino. Arguably, this *conjunto* was the most popular in Cuba in the early 1950s. It was featured daily on a major television show. The Casino traveled through Cuba every year playing at carnival venues from February to July. It seemed that almost overnight some of its tunes, often arranged by master *tres* player Niño Rivera, became national hits and classics of the decade, as in "Sun sun babae." The Casino became known for its elegant sartorial splendor, and not surprisingly, it was Patato who was in charge of the clothing worn by all band members.

The television show made Patato a household name in Cuba. His double-barrel skills as drummer and dancer defined his showmanship. He designed several very personal dance styles of his own, such as *la toalla* (the towel), *el yo-yo,* and *el tirabuzón* (the corkscrew). But the one that the audience identified most readily with Patato's performance was his rendition of *el pingüino* (the penguin dance). The catchy tune of "El pingüino" was later recorded by Tito Puente. It made a successful comeback in the mid-1980s when merengue star Johnny Ventura released a merengue version of it. "El pingüino" has also been recorded as a *cumbia.*

Patato became an idol to many young fans throughout Cuba. On one occasion, a mother brought her young five-year-old son to meet his hero Patato at the television studio. The chubby youngster would eventually grow up to be known as Changuito, today one of Cuba's leading percussionists, who expanded the role of the trap set in Cuban music. More than forty years after they first met, Patato and Changuito would get together in San Francisco to record (with Orestes Vilato) a tasty percussion CD, released in 1995.[17]

In Havana, the Conjunto Casino played in nightclubs for both locals and tourists, the latter mostly from the United States. In 1952, the Casino traveled to New York City for a three-week engagement, Patato's first visit to the United States. He was familiar with the New York music scene from conversations with expatriate Cuban musicians, such as Mongo Santamaría, when they were in Havana on vacation or visiting relatives. (In fact, visits by Mongo sometimes turned into full drumming jams.)

By 1953, Patato had become a much-sought-after percussionist for recording sessions. He recorded with many orchestras and *conjuntos,* including those led by Adolfo Guzmán, Julio Cueva, the Conjunto Baconao, and others. He led the way in the introduction of tunable metal keys for the congas. Until Patato popularized the new style, conga percussionists, for example, Chano Pozo, Mongo Santamaría, and others, had used congas with the skins nailed on to the head of the drum. This required them to light small fires or to hold candles under the open end of the drum in order to tune the sound upward. Patato's idea eliminated what was a cumbersome and even dangerous practice—especially when drummers were forced to light fires inside nightclubs or studios in order to tune their instruments.

With the help of Armando Peraza and Mongo Santamaría, Patato Valdés came to New York in 1954. For Armando he brought a gift: a handpicked conga drum from Cuba. Patato plunged right into a variety of musical activities. He played in Latin jazz groups: for the first two years he gigged on and off with Tito Puente and then joined the Machito band from 1956 to 1958. With Machito, Patato would travel to Puerto Rico, Venezuela, and Panama. He played Cuban commercial, popular music: he worked with Sexteto La Playa and recorded two albums of traditional Cuban music with Puerto Rican bandleader Luis "Lija" Ortiz. The recordings featured the Cuban-born veteran of the New York scene Panchito Riset and included the sound of Mario Bauzá on trumpet. Some of the tunes became extremely popular throughout the entire continent, in particular Panchito Riset's renditions of "El cuartito," "Blancas azucenas," and "A las seis es la cita." The albums also included "Te fuiste," a hit tune by famed percussionist Silvestre Méndez.

Patato also worked in the field of Afro-Cuban folklore: he mastered *batá* drums with the guidance of a giant in the field, Julito Collazo. With Collazo and Silvestre Méndez, and under the leadership of Mongo Santamaría, he participated in the recording of a classic album of Afro-Cuban percussion, first entitled *Changó* and later reissued as *Drums and Chants.*

And he began to play and record in the jazz idiom. He was not unfamiliar with jazz or jazz drumming styles; while still in Cuba, he had sat in with Buddy Rich of the visiting Tommy Dorsey orchestra and paired up with drummer Shelley Manne in the Woody Herman band that toured in Havana in the early 1950s. His first jazz job in the United States was with trumpeter Kenny Dorhan.[18] He recorded with Dorhan and played occasionally with the band. One memorable occasion took place at New York's Saint Nicholas Arena, where Billie Holiday sang accompanied by Dorhan's group. In those early years, Patato also played with Billy Taylor and, in 1957, recorded with Art Blakey.

In 1958, Patato Valdés teamed up with flutist Herbie Mann, with whom he would work for the next nine years. With Herbie Mann, Patato starred again as a drummer, dancer, and showman.[19] The group toured Europe and Africa. The African tour lasted four months and included visits to Liberia, Zaire/Republic of Congo, South Africa, Kenya, and Zanzibar. With Herbie Mann, Patato recorded a half-dozen LPs, including *Live at Newport* in 1963 and *Flautista! Herbie Mann Plays Afro-Cuban Jazz,* a live recording for Verve Records that featured percussionists José Luis Mangual and Santos Miranda in addition to Patato. This recording is representative of much of the work in the Herbie Mann period: Patato had carte blanche to select and play a wide variety of rhythms and drums, over which Herbie Mann laid his flute riffs. The freewheeling improvisational character of these sessions was vividly captured in the tunes "Todos Locos," "Cuban 'potato' chips," and their version of Juan Tizol's "Caravan," all on the *Flautista* album.

While playing with Herbie Mann, Patato had time to record in the Latin jazz mode with both Tito Puente and Willie Bobo. He played congas for Bobo in two collectors' albums: *One, Two, Three* and *Juicy.* He was featured in Cal Tjaders's 1966 *Soul Burst* album, which included probably the first version of Cachao's famed "Descarga cubana" by a U.S. jazz group. He also recorded with Grant Green, J. J. Johnson, Cab Calloway, Quincy Jones, and Dizzy Gillespie.

From the time of his arrival in New York in 1954, Patato and some friends would play street rumbas at New York's Central Park and other locations from time to time. Those who participated would include Héctor Cadavieco, Mario Cadavieco, Eugenio Arango, Juan

Dreke, and Tony Mayarí. These impromptu jam sessions would eventually become the masterpiece *Patato and Totico*. Released in 1968, the album featured the drumming of Patato and two other noted percussionists, Virgilio Martí and Papaíto; the singing of Totico (Eugenio Arango); the Abakuá vocals of Juan Dreke; the bass of Cachao López; and the *tres* of famed Cuban *sonero* Arsenio Rodríguez. *Patato and Totico* is the only recording that brought together Cuban masters Patato, Cachao, and Arsenio Rodríguez. The entire recording personnel played as a group only once more, one evening at New York's Corso's. Eugenio Arango would join Patato in another recording, Pupi Legarreta's *Salsa nova*. In the 1970s, Patato had a number of instructional albums as a leader for the Latin Percussion Company, including *Understanding Latin Rhythms, Vol. 1; Authority; Ready for Freddy;* and *Bata y rumba*. His work for Latin Percussion led to the organization of the Latin Percussion Jazz Ensemble, which toured Europe successfully in 1978 until its name was changed to the Tito Puente Jazz Ensemble, a change that caused Patato to quit. Patato stayed in Europe, settled in Paris for two years, and played there with Alfredo Rodriguez's Sonido Sólido band. He also appeared in Brigitte Bardot's film *And God Created Woman*. Eventually, the late Argentine pianist Jorge Dalto, who had also left the Tito Puente ensemble, asked Patato to join Dalto's Inter-American Band. With Dalto's group Patato toured Europe once again before returning to the United States in the early 1980s.

Patato became quite active after his return to the United States. First, he toured with the Machito orchestra under the direction of Machito's son, Mario Grillo, and later with Mario Bauzá's Afro-Cuban Jazz Orchestra. He participated in the 1989 San Francisco Conga Summit, which brought together Francisco Aguabella, Daniel Ponce, Julito Collazo, Cachao, and Patato. Patato also recorded several discs with Mario Bauzá: *My Time Is Now, Tanga,* and *944 Columbus*. His drums can be heard in the soundtrack of the film *The Mambo Kings,* and he also appeared in the movie *The Pusher*. A recording made in 1984, before Jorge Dalto's untimely death, was finally released in the mid-1990s with the title *Masterpiece*. Patato led Changuito and Vilató in *Ritmo y candela;* went to Europe to record, with Paquito D'Rivera and Bebo Valdés, *Bebo Rides Again;* and appeared in documentary interviews as well as instructional percussion videos.[20] Currently the leader of his own group, Afrojazzia, Carlos Valdés is regarded by his peers in Afro-Cuban percussion as a genius who not only established new conga designs but who defined the field again and again with his own unique, splendid . . . Patato style.

FRANCISCO AGUABELLA: *OLUBATÁ*

The musical biography of Francisco Aguabella bears testimony to the existence and continuity of a sacred tradition in dancing and music that has been present throughout the development of popular music in the Afro-Cuban style. A sacred drummer *(olubatá)* of the Regla de Ocha (Santería) religion, Francisco Aguabella excelled as a percussionist in Latin jazz, Latin rock, salsa, and Afro-Cuban folkloric ensembles over a thirty-five year period. His musical ideas and his vast knowledge of Cuban songs, rhythms, and styles of African origin inspired numerous recordings and performances by other musicians in the United States. He has trained a whole generation of U.S. percussionists in the secrets of Lucumí, Iyesá, Arará, Abakuá, and other Cuban rhythmic styles.

Francisco Aguabella was born in Matanzas, Cuba, on October 10, 1925, to a working-class family. His mother was a seamstress and his father worked loading sugar in a warehouse. Francisco's family was hard hit by a typhus epidemic: five of six brothers succumbed to the disease, sparing only Francisco, who was the youngest child, and an older sister. Francisco attended public schools until the tenth grade, when he went to work with his father.[21]

From a very early age, music was present in Francisco's life. From both branches of his family he was exposed to a variety of musical traditions: the *batá* drumming of the Lucumí in Santería, the parallel traditions of the Iyesá branch of Yoruba speakers, Arará (Ewe) music, and so on. An uncle played various percussion instruments locally with the orchestra of Luis Torriente. Francisco also listened to the exciting sounds of street rumba players (fig. 5).

At age twelve, Francisco began to play sacred *fundamento batá,* the three sacred drums of the Santería religion, at the urging of his older friend and mentor Esteban Vega, also known as Chacha. For two years he studied and played the sacred patterns on the *okónkolo.* He went on to play *itótele* for three additional years before a final two years of play-ing and mastering the *iyá.* At the time, there were very few *fundamento batá* drum sets in Cuba, not more than a dozen. The sacred drums in existence were directly descended from the first set ever consecrated in Cuba in the 1830s. Francisco learned his *fundamento* drumming and was "sworn to the drum" on the *batá* set that belonged to Carlos Al-fonso in Matanzas.[22]

At eighteen, Francisco joined Efí Yumane, one of the local Abakuá *juegos,* or *potencias* (societies). He became a close friend of Julito Col-lazo, another drummer and member of Efí Oronda, another local Abakuá *juego.* Francisco learned the intricacies of Abakuá drumming and became familiar as well with two less-common musical traditions in the area, the Iyesá and the Arará.

In 1947, he moved to Havana, where he worked as a longshoreman. From time to time he would travel the hundred miles back to Matanzas to work in that port loading sugar into transport ships. During the next six years, we find him working on the docks during the day and engag-ing in a variety of musical activities at night and during weekends and holidays.

He continued to work as a *fundamento* drummer for Santería cere-monies in Havana, something that forced him to learn the local idio-syncrasies of the liturgy. The remuneration for this type of activity was minimal. An *olubatá* might make, after seven or eight hours of ex-hausting exertion, no more than the equivalent of two dollars in terms of formal payment and donations. In Havana, he played *batá* with Trinidad Torregrosa, Raúl Díaz, Jesús Pérez, and other well-known

Figure 5. Francisco Aguabella. Photograph courtesy
of Katherine Hagedorn.

bataleros. He watched the legendary Pablo Roche play his *fundamento bata* in the neighboring town of Guanabacoa. Francisco played at the house of famed *santera* Pepa Echubí and participated in the yearly Yemayá procession to the Havana harbor.

Eventually, he was asked by Trinidad Torregrosa to join him, Raúl Díaz, Merceditas Valdés, and others in their *Sun sun babae* show at the Sans Souci, one of Havana's leading nightclubs of the 1940s and 1950s. At the Sans Souci show, Francisco played every form of Afro-Cuban drumming: popular rumba, *bata* rhythms, Arará, Iyesá, *bembé,* and so forth. When Trinidad Torregrosa and some members of the troupe left to take the show to Las Vegas in 1953, Francisco remained at the Sans Souci as the leader of a reorganized *Sun sun babae* show.

As soon as he arrived in Havana, Aguabella joined one of the city's most renowned carnival *comparsas,* Los Dandys de Belén. He played the lead *quinto* drum for several years and, together with another drummer (Angué, uncle of 1960s bandleader Pello el Afrokán), led the rhythm ensemble of Los Dandys. In this capacity, he became known to other local percussionists such as Patato Valdés and Mongo Santamaría. Playing for *comparsas* was exciting: for three months, street bands from working-class districts of Havana prepared methodically, hoping to win the various prizes offered to them during the carnival competitions. The days of competition were physically demanding. Drummers were required to march for hours while playing drums slung from their shoulders. Pay was minimal; a drummer might get $25 after three months of work. But it was a lot of fun. Francisco and his friends played in carnival for the love of it, not for riches.[23]

In 1953, U.S. dancer, choreographer, and anthropologist Katherine Dunham watched Francisco Aguabella's performance at the Sans Souci and immediately sought his services. Dunham had previously hired Cuban percussionists (such as Julio La Rosa), and for a time Cuban flutist and composer Gilberto Valdés had been the company's musical director. Her dance troupe was involved in making the movie *Mambo* in Rome (with Silvana Mangano, Shelley Winters, and Anthony Quinn), and she wanted to include Francisco in her company. After some hesitation, and upon the advice of his good friend Julito Collazo, Francisco decided to make the trip to Italy.

Dunham also hired the Cuban singer Xiomara Alfaro, who traveled with Francisco to New York to catch a ship to Naples. While in New York, they had the good fortune of running into Merceditas Valdés and other members of the *Sun sun babae* show who were returning to Cuba. The trip to Italy was generally uneventful, except for a prolonged bout of seasickness, which affected both Xiomara and Francisco after the ship had reached the Azores. The malady was, in their minds, connected with a serious shipwreck the previous year: the Cuban circus ship *Razzore* had sunk and its entire crew perished during a storm in the Atlantic.

The contract with Dunham called only for Francisco's participation in the activities connected with filming in Rome. The film was made. (Francisco appears briefly playing bongos at the beginning of the movie.) But his stay with the troupe became longer and longer, as Dunham would ask him repeatedly to extend his contract. So instead of returning to Cuba in three months, Francisco accompanied the dance company to Germany, where it performed in Mannheim, Düsseldorf, Frankfurt, Nuremberg, and Berlin; to France, where the show went on in Cannes and Marseille; to Monte Carlo, Monaco; to Switzerland, where they played Lausanne, Zurich, and Geneva; to Gibraltar; to Dakar, Senegal; to Brazil, Argentina, and Uruguay in South America; and to the United States, where presentations were made in Detroit, Chicago, Los Angeles, San Francisco, Las Vegas, and New York (at the Broadway Theatre for three months). Then the Dunham dancers went to Australia, where they spent fourteen months performing in Sydney, Melbourne, Adelaide, and Perth. After that came New Zealand. The original three months became four years.

Francisco enjoyed the Katherine Dunham period. He learned the intricacies of ordering food in different languages, found out that Italians didn't know how to cook rice Cuban style, and spent a generally good time with his buddy Julito Collazo, who joined the company a few months into the European trip. He played a wide variety of Cuban rhythms for the dance company as well as other Latin American styles. Haitian drummer Albert Laguerre and Francisco joined to play both Haitian and Cuban styles. And in addition to drumming, Francisco danced and acted in some of Dunham's choreographed dances. He also met Marbel Martin, to whom he became engaged. When the dance company dissolved in 1957, Francisco married Marbel and settled in the United States.

During his first few years in the United States, Francisco's knowledge and skill produced an immediate impact. He recorded with Tito Puente on the LP *Top Percussion,* which included Mongo Santamaría, Willie Bobo, Julito Collazo, and Marcelino Guerra. Francisco introduced two Iyesá tunes in that album, "Obatalá Yeza" and "Alaumba Chemache."[24] He wrote two other *guaguancó* tunes, "Complicación" and "Agua limpia," which were recorded by Tito Puente on the 1957 *Dancemania* LP. They would be sung by Carlos Embale on the 1959 classic recording *Mongo in Havana: Bembé,* recorded in Havana, featuring Mongo, Carlos Embale, Merceditas Valdés, Willie Bobo, and several outstanding local musicians.

But Francisco preferred the more relaxed ambiance of the West Coast to what he perceived to be the intense, sometimes aggressive milieu of New York City. He worked with René Touzet in Los Angeles in 1959 (at the Crescendo in Manhattan Beach), performed with the Durán brothers at the Copacabana in San Francisco, and toured Japan with Pérez Prado, all while starting a family.

While moving back and forth between San Francisco and Los Angeles, Francisco joined Mongo Santamaría and other percussionists on two albums of classic Cuban rhythms produced by Fantasy. The first, *Yambú,* was recorded in 1958 and featured, besides Mongo and Francisco, Pablo Mozo, Willie Bobo, Carlos Vidal, Modesto Durán, Al McKibbon, Israel del Pino, and Mercedes Hernández. Aguabella contributed the tunes "Macunsere," "Brícamo," and "Longoíto," among others. The second album was *Mongo,* recorded in 1959, with two tunes by Francisco, "Ayenye" and "Onyaye." Besides the personnel from *Yambú,* an additional top percussionist, Armando Peraza, was added as well as Vince Guaraldi and José "Chombo" Silva on the tune "Mazacote."

Because of the success of these albums, Fantasy contracted Francisco to produce an album under his own name, *Dance the Latin Way,* which came out in 1962. While not a national success, it did sell thirty-five thousand copies. During these years, Francisco acquired formal Western art music training, learning to read music and play the acoustic bass, and performed at jazz festivals with Dizzy Gillespie and Cal Tjader.

Introduced to Peggy Lee by Dizzy Gillespie, Francisco would work steadily with her until 1969. He played congas, bongos, timpani, and every form of percussion. For several years he accompanied Peggy on nationwide tours that usually lasted three weeks. While in New York, he would jam occasionally with Eddie Palmieri. During those years he also recorded with Benny Carter, Nancy Wilson, Lalo Schiffrin, the Jazz Crusaders, the Mary Kay Trio, Three Dog Night, Al Hirt, Emil Richards, Dinah Shore, Tito Rodriguez, and Don Ellis (for the movie soundtrack of *French Connection II*).

After leaving Peggy Lee, Aguabella joined Frank Sinatra, with whom he played in Las Vegas and toured the United States.[25] Finally tired of touring, Francisco returned to the Bay Area in 1969, where he hooked up with Luis Gasca and other Latino musicians interested in rock music. Eventually these musicians would coalesce around Jorge Santana's MALO, a band that shone with intensity from 1971 until its demise in 1974. With MALO, Francisco once again toured all over the United States (the first tour alone was forty-two one-nighters) and recorded three albums. The band played not only for youthful audiences interested in Latin rock but for older, traditional dances, such as the memorable New Year's Eve Dance at the Long Beach Sports Arena in 1973. In all instances, Francisco's powerful, explosive style on either four or five conga drums dominated the rhythm section.

After the breakup of MALO, Francisco toured for a while with Weather Report, joined Cal Tjader at the Santa Barbara Jazz Festival, and recorded with Joe Henderson in San Francisco. In 1975, we find him at the Monterey Jazz Festival with Dizzy Gillespie and performing again with Frank Sinatra in Las Vegas. He toured briefly with Carlos Santana in Canada in 1976. And in 1978, he participated in the recording of the classic album of Cuban percussion mentioned earlier, *Ekué Ritmos Cubanos,* with Louie Bellson, Walfredo de los Reyes, Alex Acuña, Cachao, Manolo Badrena, Luis Conte, Cat Anderson, and Lou Tabackin. He played with both Dizzy and Machito at the 1978 Santa Barbara Jazz Festival. In 1977 and 1978, his long-term association with Eddie Palmieri led to the production of two important albums that featured Aguabella's drumming, *Lucumí Macumba Voudou* and *Justicia.*

In the early 1980s, Aguabella remained for the most part in San Francisco. There followed a number of years of intense activity in the Bay Area. Francisco became the main attraction at the renowned Caesars Palace in the Mission District, where many memorable jam sessions took place. At the same time, he took up the mission of teaching the *fundamento batá* drumming to avid students. His first three students from that period, John Santos, Harold Muñiz, and Michael Spiro, went on to become influential figures in the Bay Area music scene in the next decade. With them and others, Francisco traveled back and forth, playing at ceremonies in both the Los Angeles and San Francisco areas.

In 1985, the impact of Francisco's artistry came to the attention of noted filmmaker Les Blank, who began to work on a documentary on Aguabella's life. The film *(Sworn to the Drum),* which was finally released in 1995, utilizes footage from two important dates. The first was the 1985 tribute to Francisco Aguabella at Caesars Palace, which featured Julito Collazo, Armando Peraza, Carlos Santana, Sheila Escovedo, and a folkloric group under Francisco's direction. The second, in the fall of 1986, was the Conga Summit that Francisco organized, in which Daniel Ponce, Patato Valdés, Cachao, and other musicians participated.

In the more commercial realm, Francisco's activities diminished somewhat during those years, although he recorded with Tito Puente the *El rey* album at the Great American Music Hall for Concord Records. He also joined Max Roach, Philly Joe Jones, Shelley Manne, Billy Higgins, and Babatunde Olatunje for the 1984 Watts Drum Festival.

In the late 1980s, Aguabella relocated to Los Angeles, where once again he has been active as a bandleader of both salsa and Latin jazz groups, and where he continues to teach (one of his students is noted ethnomusicologist Katherine Hagedorn) and to play the *batá* drums for ceremonies and *bembés*. His tune "Pronto salsa" appeared as part of the *Music from the Streets of Los Angeles* CD released by Rhythm Safari in 1991. His own folkloric group released a recording, *Oriza,* in 1992. In late 1995, he traveled to the Bay Area to participate in a tribute to Armando Peraza and recorded with Mongo Santamaría, Poncho Sánchez, and Al McKibbon. Francisco participated in the Los Angeles Latin Jazz Festivals in 1997 and 1998. He recorded two CDs, *H2O* and *Agua de Cuba,* which were released at end of the 1990s.

In 1992, the National Endowment for the Arts awarded Francisco Aguabella a National Heritage Fellowship in recognition of his lifelong dedication to music.[26] And in 1995, his folkloric ensemble was featured at the national meeting of the Society for Ethnomusicology in Los Angeles.

Francisco Aguabella has kept alive the rich drumming traditions that evolved in Cuba from earlier African traditions. He has played an important role in maintaining and developing that musical idiom in the Los Angeles and San Francisco areas. He continues to teach and perform actively. What Peraza did for the bongos and Patato for the congas, Aguabella did for the sacred *batá* drums in the United States.

CÁNDIDO CAMERO: THE CANDY MAN

To complete an account of the contribution of Afro-Cuban percussionists to jazz and Latin jazz, one must include the name of Cándido

Camero Guerra. In a career that spanned more than fifty years, Cándido performed and recorded with more than one hundred top artists in the field of jazz throughout the world. More than any other percussionist of his generation, Cándido succeeded in making the sound of the conga drums a standard coloration in straight-ahead jazz rhythm sections.

Cándido Camero was born in the small town of San Antonio de los Baños, in the province of Havana, very near the capital city of Cuba. His parents, Cándido Camero and Caridad Guerra, were of humble origin, but there was a strong musical tradition on both sides of his family. Thus, although the young Cándido never had formal music training, he grew familiar with the instruments of the Cuban *son* from an early age. At four, he was already beginning to play bongos under the tutelage of his maternal uncle, Andrés Guerra. His own father began to teach him the secrets of the *tres* guitar when Cándido Jr. was a mere eight years old.[27]

Cándido was still very young when his family moved to Havana, to the El Cerro district. His early acquaintance with the *tres* allowed him to secure a job in 1935 playing this instrument with a premiere *son* septet, the Gloria Habanera. Soon he went on to play with other important music groups in Havana. Some of these included groups led by Tata Gutiérrez and Bienvenido León, as well as the famed Sonora Piñón. Cándido played *tres* for these groups but also continued to play percussion instruments. He was a drummer for the outstanding El Alacrán *comparsa* during the yearly Havana carnivals, for example.[28]

Cándido's recognition as a prominent and tasty *tres* player led no less than Arsenio Rodríguez to select him as the *tres* player and group leader for the Conjunto Segundo Arsenio. This group filled in for Arsenio's regular *conjunto* and played the same repertoire when the heavy demand for Arsenio's *conjunto* made it impossible for one group to cover all the dates. His equally remarkable dexterity as a percussionist allowed him to join the show orchestra of the famed Tropicana cabaret, where he played both bongos and congas.

It was his reputation as a percussionist that allowed him to travel to the United States for the first time in 1946. He came to New York as part of the accompaniment of the show-dance couple Carmen y Rolando, which performed at two well-known venues, the Havana Madrid and La Conga Club. The initial contract called for a twelve-week engagement, but the success of the troupe led to repeated renewals until the stay had lasted a full year. Cándido returned to Cuba but then joined the Billy Taylor Trio in 1950 for a one-and-a-half-year stint in the the United States. After successfully recording and performing with Taylor, Cándido was back in Havana in 1952, where he was once again the featured *conguero* at the Tropicana cabaret. It was during this period of back-and-forth travel between the Big Apple and the Pearl of the Antilles that Cándido joined, along with many other Havana musicians, the *batanga* rhythm experiment initiated by Bebo Valdés in Havana. He took part as well in films that featured Cuba's music life.[29]

In 1953, Cándido was back in the United States, where he continued to play and record with the most prominent and innovative jazz musicians of that age, including Dizzy Gillespie and Charlie Parker. That same year, he became the first Afro-Cuban percussionist to record with British pianist George Shearing for his "Latin" debut album, *Latin Satin*. After Shearing, Cándido moved on to join the Stan Kenton Orchestra, with which he played for several years. In great demand as a Latin percussionist sideman, Cándido performed and recorded with a large number of jazz artists during this time. A prominent example came in 1956, when the great Duke Ellington and Billy Strayhorn wrote their "Drum Is a Woman" suite, which featured Cándido Camero on Afro-Cuban percussion (fig. 6).

In the early 1960s, Cándido led his own quintet—which featured the newly arrived Cachao López—playing at El Liborio and the Chateau Madrid in New York City. He also participated, playing both congas and bongos, in the legendary *descargas* at the Village Gate in 1966, which brought together the best Latin musicians of New York City

Figure 6. Cándido Camero. Photograph by Enid Farber.

(Eddie and Charlie Palmieri, Bobby Rodriguez, Cachao, Ray Barreto, Joe Cuba, Tito Puente, Chocolate, Chino Pozo, Monguito, Chivirico, and Cheo Feliciano) for a series of jam sessions of a genre that was not then known as salsa. Of course, in the 1970s Cándido would perform often with the most representative New York salsa ensemble, the Fania All-Stars. He also joined Charles Mingus for the latter's fusion experiment combining *cumbia*—Colombia's Afro-based national dance— with jazz.

Over the last twenty-five years, Cándido has continued to build on his already established reputation as a well-rounded percussionist. His complete list of recordings as a sideman is awesome. It includes more than one hundred credits, which include, in addition to the artists already mentioned, sessions with Woody Herman, Art Blakey, Wes Montgomery, Kenny Clarke, Ray Charles, Kenny Burrell, Tony Bennett, Erroll Garner, Dinah Washington, Sonny Rollins, Stan Getz,

Elvin Jones, Buddy Rich, and Count Basie. Those, of course, are only a partial list of his jazz and pop record credits. He remained equally active as a percussionist in the purely Afro-Cuban field, working over his decades-long career with Machito, Joe Loco, Miguelito Valdés, Mongo Santamaría, and Chico O'Farrill in addition to his early work with Bebo Valdés. He also led his own group for a while and recorded under his own name. *Brujerías de Cándido,* which features Cachao López among others, was released to relative success in 1973.

Cándido's greatest contribution was establishing the conga drums as an integral, if not essential, component of the modern straight-ahead jazz percussion scheme and securing a place for the "Latin tinge" among the many rhythmic tinges available to the modern jazz drummer.

While Peraza, Aguabella, and Patato remained associated for relatively long periods of time to a few bandleaders, Cándido's career was remarkably different in that he collaborated with such a large number of different leaders. His compatriots were perhaps more central to the development of Latin jazz as a new fusion; yet Cándido's early collaboration with George Shearing and, later, the *cumbia* jazz experiment with Charles Mingus must be counted as milestones in the development of Latin jazz styles. Taken together, Peraza, Patato, Aguabella, Cándido, and, of course, Mongo Santamaría provided a sound foundation for the continued expansion of that hybrid of hybrids, Latin jazz.

CHAPTER SEVEN

Chocolate Dreams

The name of Alfredo "Chocolate" Armenteros has become synonymous in the United States with the traditional, or *típico,* style of Cuban
trumpet playing. In contrast to jazz, which favors harmonic improvisation, the power and depth of Cuban rhythms is such that it defines the
improvisational styles of melody instruments such as trumpets, flutes,
trombones, saxophones, and so forth. By extension, melody instrumentalists in Latin jazz often incorporate rhythmic phrasing, diction, and
improvisation in their compositions and performances. Of the countless fine Cuban melody instrumentalists, Chocolate presents one of the
most interesting examples because of his unique musical history. Over
the course of his illustrious career, he was a lead trumpet player for the
1940s creator of the *son montuno,* Arsenio Rodríguez; for the giant of
Cuba's 1950s dance music, Beny Moré; and for the founding orchestra
of New York's Afro-Cuban jazz, Machito and the Afro-Cubans.

For over six decades, he has played Cuban music with the leading
exponents of its varied genres, in and outside Cuba: in addition to playing and recording with Rodríguez, Moré, and Machito, he figured
prominently in the recordings of Fajardo, Sexteto La Playa, Harlow,
Eddie Palmieri, Charlie Palmieri, Cachao, Mongo Santamaría, and the
Sonora Mantancera. Furthermore, Chocolate has been the leader of his

own ensembles. He has been featured in innumerable radio and television shows, concerts, and other live performances. A down-to-earth and good-humored artist, Chocolate has been a goodwill ambassador for Cuban music throughout Mexico, Venezuela, Puerto Rico, Haiti, and Colombia, as well as in the United States, where he makes his residence.

Alfredo Armenteros was born on April 4, 1928, in the rural town of Ranchuelo, in central Cuba near the city of Cienfuegos. His father, Genaro, owned a grocery store, while his mother, Angelina, kept house. His paternal great-grandfather, Simeón Armenteros, was a general in the Revolutionary Army during Cuba's War of Independence against Spain.[1]

The young Alfredo was exposed to a variety of musical experiences. His father had been a trombone player before dedicating himself full-time to business. Moreover, Ranchuelo was a unique city in that the head of the largest employer, cigarette-maker Amado Trinidad Velasco, promoted musical activities for personal and business reasons. Trinidad had invested heavily in a national radio broadcasting company that vied for first place in popular ratings. To attract a larger audience, Trinidad sponsored many new and upcoming musicians, *conjuntos,* and orchestras which, to the great fortune of young Alfredo, performed in Ranchuelo. Chocolate remembers attending performances as a child and teenager of the likes of Arsenio Rodríguez, Arcaño, Celia Cruz, Hermanos Lebatard, Mariano Mercerón, and many others. Visiting groups played Cuban music for the most part but also the better-known international melodies and jazz tunes (fig. 7).

While still in grade school, Alfredo began to take trumpet lessons with Eduardo Egües, father of the flutist of Orquesta Aragón, Richard Egües. Whatever he learned, Alfredo taught in turn to his cousin Armando Armenteros, who also went on to become a leading trumpeter.[2] Armando, who played drums in a city marching band, likewise showed Alfredo the rhythm patterns for his instrument. The young Alfredo

Figure 7. Chocolate Armenteros *(left)* with author.
Personal collection of the author.

also routinely attended a wide variety of Afro-Cuban celebrations, which acquainted him thoroughly with the percussion styles characteristic of these traditions. This knowledge was easily acquired, as the Cabildo de Santa Bárbara, run by local folks of Kongo origin, was located right in front of his house in Ranchuelo.

As he studied more, Alfredo began to show a preference for the tenor sax and the trumpet. Eventually, he became familiar with the trumpet sounds of two legendary musicians, Chappottín and Florecita (Enrique Velasco), who performed often in Ranchuelo. Alfredo enjoyed listening—on his father's Victrola—to the minimalist tones of the former and the florid excursions of the latter. Soon Alfredo made up his mind that the trumpet would be his instrument. He began to develop his own style, influenced by, yet very distinct from, those of Chappottín and Florecita. Alfredo began playing with a local *conjunto,* Los Jóvenes Alegres, and with out-of-town groups such as Sagua la Grande's Hermanos García orchestra. He played in the provincial capital, Santa Clara, with the *charanga* Hijos de Arcaño, which featured Rolando LaSerie on percussion.

Chocolate's first trip to Cuba's capital of Havana took place in February of 1949, at the time of the yearly carnival celebrations. He traveled as a member of a Cienfuegos *comparsa* (street band) sponsored by a popular soft-drink company (Refresco Ironbeer). The Cienfuegos *comparsa* stood out in the carnivals because it had a new sound: two trumpets instead of the traditional one-trumpet (plus drums) orchestration of the street bands. One of the trumpets was, of course, Alfredo Armenteros, then only twenty years old.[3] And when his childhood idol Florecita fell ill, Armenteros was called to replace him on the roster of famed Havana *comparsa* La Jardinera. What was originally planned as a two-day carnival excursion turned into a two-and-half week stay and ample exposure for the young man from Ranchuelo.

Alfredo went back briefly to his hometown, but upon turning twenty-one, hoping to succeed as a professional musician, he moved to Havana. It had been twenty years since the trumpet had migrated from its earlier association with street *comparsas* to become a standard instrument in *son*-playing septets and *conjuntos.* That was the situation when Chocolate departed from Ranchuelo. He arrived in Havana on April 19, 1949, and began to work immediately. His first gigs were with the Septeto Habanero playing for dancing at the Marte y Belona Dance Academy. The next month he made his first recording, which included the tune "Para las niñas y señoras" and several others, with the René Alvarez Conjunto Los Astros.

At the Marte y Belona Academy, Chocolate befriended musicians such as Luis Martínez Griñán, known as Lilí, pianist for Arsenio Rodríguez. Playing with Arsenio had long been a dream for Chocolate. It was Arsenio who had first successfully integrated the *tumbadora,* or conga, with the traditional bongos to produce a new style of playing the *son.* And his approach was part of the musical revolution that culminated in Pérez Prado's mambo craze of the early fifties. The dream came true: after Arsenio had heard the sound of Chocolate's trumpet with René Alvarez, he approached Chocolate with his trumpeter, Félix Chappottín, who asked if Chocolate would be interested in playing with Arsenio's *conjunto.*

He played with Arsenio at the Jardines de la Polar beer gardens where Arsenio, Arcaño y Sus Maravillas, and René Alvarez alternated playing in adjacent ballrooms. Chocolate also played in radio broadcasts with the *conjunto* and recorded two tunes, "Me boté de guaño," a song about a tough guy dedicated to him by Arsenio, who also listed Chocolate as the composer, and "Yo no puedo comer vistagacha." He spent four to five months with the Arsenio Rodríguez *conjunto,* where he honed his approach to the *son,* surrounded as he was by players of the caliber of Chappottín, Lilí, and the marvelous blind *tres* player Arsenio Rodríguez himself.

Julio Gutiérrez's big band hired Chocolate away from Arsenio. This group worked a radio show for Radio Cadena Habana, where it provided accompaniment to a variety of vocalists (among others, Rita Montaner, René Cabell, and Manolo Fernández) who sang anything from Afro-Cuban themes to boleros and Argentine tangos. Alfredo— who began to be called Chocolate around this time after someone confused him for Cuban boxing champion Kid Chocolate—also played, along with pianist Pedro Jústiz ("Peruchín"), in the Campoamor Theatre Orchestra, led by Armando Romeu. Chocolate found in these early days another trumpeter who provided musical stimulus, noted Cuban jazz band and classical player Luis Escalante.

In 1950, Chocolate joined a group led by *bongosero* Cándido Requena for a three-month stint in Port-au-Prince, Haiti. Others in the group were Rolando LaSerie and pianist Omar Brito. In Haiti, Chocolate played Cuban music and learned something about the country's popular sounds—he made a recording with a local band—and traditional drumming.

This was a time of rapid deployments in the young musician's life. He returned to Havana to work with the Mariano Mercerón orchestra, and with their pianist, Peruchín, in radio station CMQ's broadcasts of *El show de la mañana;* there were gigs at the fabled Tropicana nightclub and then another international trek, this time to Venezuela. Along with another outstanding Cuban trumpet player, Alejandro "El Negro" Vivar,[4] and Manolo Manrique, the vocalist of the Hermanos Palau orchestra, Chocolate traveled to Maracaibo for the opening of the Ondas del Lago radio station. He ended up staying for six months, working with the orchestra of Puerto Rico's César Concepción. The year was 1951.

Back in Havana, Chocolate worked with the orchestra of Bebo Valdés—one of the most complete Cuban musicians of all time, father of Irakere's Chucho Valdés—when the latter introduced *batá* drums in his groundbreaking *ritmo batanga.* Others that participated in these important sessions—broadcast on radio station RHC–Cadena Azul—included El Negro Vivar, with whom Chocolate engaged in memorable *mano-a-mano* trumpet solos, and Beny Moré, who during these sessions was first referred to as the "Bárbaro del Ritmo."[5]

With the Bebo Valdés Orchestra, Chocolate accompanied visiting Colombian clarinetist Lucho Bermúdez and vocalist Matilde Díaz. Chocolate's trumpet was there in their first recordings of "Prende la vela," "Sal si puedes," and "San Fernando." He also had an opportunity to record with one of Cuba's most renowned *guajira* singers, the late Cheo Marquetti.[6]

In 1953, Chocolate was called on to replace longtime Sonora Matancera trumpeter Calixto Leicea, disabled for several months on account of illness. Chocolate teamed up with the other trumpeter, Pedro Knight, and accompanied the Sonora Matancera on their first trip outside of Cuba. The popular *conjunto* traveled to the Venezuela carnivals and to the islands of Aruba, Bonaire, and Curaçao. It was during his brief stay with the Sonora Matancera that their first recording of Oscar Boufartique's "Burundanga," featuring Celia Cruz as the vocalist, was made. Chocolate was still with the Sonora when the *conjunto* was featured for the first time in a film.

A second dream was about to come true for Chocolate: to play with the most popular dance orchestra of the Cuba of the 1950s. His cousin Beny Moré—already well known as a successful singer with the Trío Matamoros, the Conjunto de Humberto Cané, Mariano Mercerón, and the Pérez Prado mambo ensemble—asked his help in putting together a band that could substitute for the Sonora Matancera for a two-week period in a popular radio sitcom that was broadcast nationally.

Chocolate helped Beny recruit the members of the band. Beny Moré's radio stint was so successful that he was persuaded to maintain the orchestra on a regular basis. The Orquesta Gigante de Beny Moré made its debut at a dance in the town of Placetas on August 1, 1953. Soon they would record two tunes: "A la bahía de Manzanillo" and "Oye esta canción para tí." A succession of hit dance tunes would follow.

For the next three years, Chocolate worked steadily with Beny Moré as musical director of the orchestra. They played up and down the island for dances and on nationally broadcast radio programs, appeared on television, and traveled to Colombia, where they played in several venues, including the Club Campestre de Medellín.[7] Beny More's own tune, "Bonito y sabroso," was the theme song for the orchestra. Their live shows consisted normally of two sets. The first set, directed by Chocolate, featured either instrumental music or the vocals of Rolando LaSerie and Fernando Alvarez; the second set was completely the domain of the inimitable performer, conductor, composer, and vocalist Beny Moré. Sometimes the Beny Moré orchestra would take turns at live dances with other groups, such as the Conjunto Casino or the Rumbavana. Without a doubt, Moré's orchestra represented the most advanced and complex sound in Cuban music in the 1950s.

In the mid-fifties, Chocolate also made a number of recordings with José Fajardo's *charangas.* This type of Cuban orchestra enjoyed a great revival in the 1950s. The cha-cha-cha had made its flute-and-violin sound popular once again. And *charangas,* normally associated with the *danzón* genre, had expanded their repertoire and begun to play the Cuban *son* with determination. Fajardo had known Chocolate since the mid-forties, when during visits to Ranchuelo, he had marveled at the addition of trumpets (one of them Chocolate, of course) to the typical instrumentation of the *charangas.*

In early 1956, Chocolate traveled with Fajardo y Sus Estrellas to New York City for the first time. It was a one-night engagement at the Waldorf Astoria Hotel. The members of the band included Tata Güines, Ulpiano Díaz, and Félix Reina. Armenteros visited the Palladium and sat in for a couple of tunes with Machito's Afro-Cubans. He returned briefly to Havana and was then back in New York City six weeks later with Fajardo for a two-week contract at the Puerto Rico Theatre, where Fajardo and Cortijo y Su Combo played for dancing. With Cuban singer Vicentico Valdés as tour guide, Chocolate got to know the city. He played with Machito several times and saw Tito Rodríguez and Tito Puente in action.

The second visit convinced Chocolate that he wanted to come to work in New York City. He returned to Havana, got his papers in order, and was back to New York in April of 1957, hired by Palladium Enterprises. His first job in New York was with César Concepción, with whom he had already played in Venezuela back in 1951. In 1958, Chocolate became a regular member of the Machito orchestra.

He spent several years with Machito, with whom he visited Las Vegas, Panama, and Venezuela; they also went to Japan for a three-and-a-half month stint in 1962. Chocolate became thoroughly exposed to the sound of jazz, as the Machito orchestra alternated at Birdland with the likes of Dizzy Gillespie, Count Basie, and Miles Davis. At the Apollo Theatre, Machito alternated with John Coltrane, and Chocolate once accompanied Oscar Brown. During this period, Chocolate recorded with Septeto La Playa as well as with Mongo Santamaría—two tunes on *Mongo Introduces La Lupe*—and Machito.

By now, Chocolate was a much sought-after trumpeter in New York City. He played the 1963 New York World's Fair with Pacheco. He was one of the feature stars in the memorable *Descargas at the Village Gate* in 1966. That year, Chocolate began playing with Larry Harlow, with whom he recorded a number of LPs, including *Heavy Smokin, Baján-dote, Las luces,* and *El exigente,* with singer Ismael Miranda. In 1967, he was in Puerto Rico for three months, playing with a reduced lineup of the Machito orchestra at the Bar el Chico in the Hotel San Juan. With this group he visited Haiti for the second time in his life for a two-week engagement. He recorded with Mon Rivera, Moncho Leña, and Sexteto La Playa, performing a potpourri of boleros with sextet vocalist Vitín Avilés.

Chocolate had, as did many Latin musicians in the United States, his share of dry times when there no jobs available in the music business. For a while he worked in a cleaning business, driving a delivery truck. And often he made money playing jingles, nothing fancy. Chocolate recorded a couple of those for Cuban arranger Chico O'Farrill.

In the late 1960s and early 1970s, Armenteros began to work with Eddie Palmieri. With Palmieri he visited Colombia twice, in trips that took him to Bogotá, Cali, Buenaventura, and other cities. He performed at live concerts at Attica prison, at Sing Sing, and at the University of Puerto Rico. He and Eddie also jointly composed their famous tune "Chocolate Ice Cream." In 1974, Choco—as he is affectionately known—began a five-year association with the Sonora Matancera, with whom he traveled to Mexico, Santo Domingo, Colombia, Chile, Peru, and Puerto Rico. His recordings with the Sonora included the hit "Mala mujer." In the same year, he began to play with Charlie Palmieri, with whom he recorded "La hija de Lola."

A third dream of Chocolate's came true in 1974 as well. For the first time, he recorded under his own name. The LP *Chocolate aquí* featured

Marcelino Guerra (Rapindey) and Justo Betancourt on vocals as well as Nicki Marrero, Andy Gonzalez, and Julito Collazo.

Three years later, Chocolate participated in the *Concepts in Unity* recordings of the Grupo Folklórico Experimental Nuevayorquino. This historic recording grew out of informal gatherings and *descargas* by New York's finest Puerto Rican, Cuban, and other musicians with a Latin bent, energized by noted Cuban music collector-historian René López. Chocolate shined in his playing of "Choco's *Guajira,*" a tune that would become firmly associated with the sound of his trumpet. In the same year, 1977, Chocolate was present at the tribute to Cachao organized by René Hernández at the Avery Fisher Hall in New York City.

In the 1980s, Chocolate joined the project, initiated by Cuban *sonero* Roberto Torres, designed to focus and revive the Cuban *típico* sound in New York via recordings on the SAR label. With Roberto Torres and Alfredito Valdés Jr., he traveled to central Africa, Cameroon, Gabon, and Senegal. Featuring Chocolate's trumpet, a number of recordings came out of this tour and are available on CD as *The Best of Chocolate,* volumes 1 and 2. The material is interesting because these *típico* Cuban players adopted a slower and sweeter mode of playing the *son cubano,* more appealing to the ears of their contemporary African audiences.

Chocolate joined Machito again in 1979 and remained in Europe (living in Spain, where his cousin and only direct disciple on the trumpet, Armando Armenteros, lives and works) after Machito's death in London in 1984. In the mid-eighties, Chocolate released a recording with a Latin jazz approach that showcased his gifted playing of Cuban genres: *Chocolate en septeto* amounts to a clinic in which Choco demonstrates his approach to the *son,* the *guajira,* the *guaguancó,* the *pregón,* and the *bolero.* A few years later, two other recordings, *Rompiendo el hielo* and *Chocolate y amigos,* were also released.

In the last few years, Chocolate has slowed down his professional activity. But he continues to record; his sound can be heard in recent releases by Paquito D'Rivera, Poncho Sánchez, the Machete Ensemble, Ramón Veloz Jr., and the two *Master Sessions* by Cachao. He has recently released two CDs under his own name. He appeared prominently in Andy Garcia's documentary *Como mi ritmo no hay dos*.

Alfredo "Chocolate" Armenteros stands out as one of the exemplary trumpet players in a musical tradition where the trumpet is as ubiquitous as the conga drum. Among trumpeters, Choco was certainly the one who took the Cuban sound to all corners of the globe: from Tokyo to Cotonou, from Chile to Finland; he was also the one who most often recorded Cuban music with the widest variety of ensembles. After the deaths of Alejandro "El Negro" Vivar and Jorge Varona, Chocolate remains the link between the age in which the trumpet *típico* sound developed in the music ensembles of Arsenio Rodríguez, Julio Cueva, and Beny Moré and the next generations of trumpeters: Mirabal, Sandoval, Munguía, and Alemañy.

CHAPTER EIGHT

The Taste of *¡Azúcar!*

There is no doubt that Celia Cruz was a central figure for understanding the popularity of Cuban music, the growth of salsa, and, indirectly, the development of Latin jazz. The day Celia Cruz passed away—July 16, 2003, in New York City—millions of people throughout the world mourned her death. The pope, the king and queen of Spain, Latin American presidents, the mayor of New York City, the governor of New York, and both New York state senators expressed their condolences through official messages. On the day of her funeral, her remains were carried in a horse-drawn carriage for thirty blocks down Fifth Avenue to a solemn and grandiose mass at New York's Saint Patrick's Cathedral. In previous days, more than one hundred thousand mourners had paid their respects to her at funeral homes in Miami and New York City.

Luck alone cannot account for the impact of her music and her immense popularity. Celia Cruz had a great voice and an even greater presence on the stage. But it was her involvement in artistic decisions, her selection of tunes for performance and recording, her direct intervention in every detail of her recordings, and her choice of musicians (many of whom she made famous) that made her into one of the founders of a music with worldwide impact. Her contribution was all the more noteworthy because she made it in a music genre that was acutely male-dominated.

Her musical labors directly contributed to the gradual spread and transformation of what has become a hybridized Cuban music. This transculturation has given Latin Americans from a host of countries, as well as those who live in Latin diasporic communities in North America and Europe, a sense of pride, solidarity, and collective pleasure. They recognize in the music of Celia Cruz an aspect of their inheritance that is genuine, modern, and without match.

Celia Cruz was born in a working-class *solar* (tenement house) in the Santos Suárez district of Havana on October 21, probably in 1920.[1] Her father, Simón Cruz, worked for the railroad. Her mother, Catalina Alfonso, took care of the house chores. Celia's maternal grandfather, Don Ramón Alfonso, was a member of the Revolutionary Army that fought against Spain during Cuba's War of Independence. There were four children in the family: Dolores, the oldest; Celia; and her younger siblings, Bárbaro and Gladys (fig. 8).

Celia attended school at Escuela Pública No. 6, República de México, which was within walking distance of her home. Because of the particular theme of the school, Celia learned at an early age to sing the national anthems of both Mexico and Cuba. Brought up Catholic, she took her First Communion at the Iglesia La Milagrosa in the Santos Suárez district.[2] Once finished with elementary school, Celia enrolled in a Catholic academy run by the Oblate Sisters, where she studied typing, shorthand, and English. Shortly thereafter, she attended normal school, where she obtained her elementary school teaching credential.

From an early age, Celia was surrounded by a rich and varied musical milieu. The Santos Suárez district, like all barrios of Havana, proudly organized a yearly carnival street band, La Jornalera. She became accustomed to the sounds of the trumpets, bells, and drums of carnival and to the music from neighborhood *bembés*. Many of her neighbors were musicians by trade. As radio broadcasts developed in Cuba in the 1920s and 1930s, Celia enjoyed listening to the music and

Figure 8. Celia Cruz. Photograph © Mark Holston.

voices of Abelardo Barroso, Fernando Collazo, Pablo Quevedo, Arsenio Rodríguez, and Arcaño y Sus Maravillas. One woman vocalist in particular caught her attention: the "Empress of the *Danzonete,*" Paulina Alvarez.

As a teenager Celia, with her girlfriends, frequented Havana's popular dance academies, such as the Antilla and the Jóvenes del Vals, where she first watched a performance by Arcaño y Sus Maravillas.[3] She always loved to sing. Celia helped her mother put her younger siblings to sleep by singing them lullabies. She intoned the melodies so beautifully with her deep voice that the neighbors would gather to hear her sing. Her alert cousin Serafín soon was encouraging her to participate in amateur contests for vocalists, popular at Havana radio stations in the 1930s.

THE EARLY YEARS

The global economic crisis of the 1930s affected Cuba deeply. Poverty and unemployment reached extreme levels. For the poor, amateur artistic competitions at radio stations became attractive because they offered the promise of useful prizes, such as baskets of food, boxes of condensed milk, and the like. Celia Cruz entered her first contest at Radio García Serra, located in the adjacent district of La Víbora. For the first round of the competition, she sang a popular tango, "Nostalgia," accompanying herself with a pair of claves in the manner of her idol Paulina Alvarez. She received a cake as a prize and made it successfully to the second, final round. Three weeks later, Celia won the final round as well and received a new prize, this time a silver necklace. By then she was singing regularly with a group from the Santos Suárez area named El Botón de Oro, led by a local *marimbulero,* Francisco Gavilán. The ensemble played for neighborhood parties and celebrations.[4]

After her initial radio success, Celia Cruz actively sought other opportunities. In 1938, she made the first cut for a more significant amateur event. An important Havana radio station, Radio Lavín, organized a contest entitled Kings of the Conga. (The conga was the dance rage at that time.) The select jury included a famed Cuban diva, Rita Montaner; composer and orchestra conductor Gonzalo Roig (author of the famed "Quiéreme Mucho" ["Yours"]); and maestro Rodrigo Prats. These three distinguished panelists chose Celia Cruz as the Queen of the Conga, the first of many "royal" titles she would acquire in subsequent years.[5]

The newly crowned young singer decided next to enter the most competitive of all radio amateur contests in Cuba, a program named *La corte suprema del arte* (The Supreme Court of Art), the only one broadcast to a national audience by radio station CMQ in Havana.[6] Celia competed with two songs: first, "Arrepentida," and a second tune, "Mango mangüé," in a duo with another young vocalist, Vilma Valle.[7] Celia and Vilma obtained a first prize for their joint effort in "Mango mangüé."

BEFORE THE SONORA MATANCERA

Shortly afterward, Celia began to work regularly at the CMQ radio station. She was featured as one of several young vocalists who sang live for a national audience accompanied by the station's orchestra every Sunday afternoon. The name of the program was *Stars Being Born.* While the pay was minimal, this job would prove, in the long run, to have been a positive step simply because Celia's voice could be heard by the entire listening audience of the island on a consistent basis.

Meanwhile, on the heels of the grave capitalist global crisis of 1930 came World War II. With the outbreak of hostilities, the island's economy, which had begun a slow recovery at the end of the 1930s, experienced a setback in its foreign trade. Economically speaking, Cuba was a kind of colony of the United States that depended substantially on active commercial relations with its powerful neighbor to the north. The naval war made it both difficult and dangerous to ship raw sugar from Cuba to the United States. At the same time, the inflow of tourists from the United States—another way in which the Cuban economy depended on the United States—was deeply affected by fear of German submarines in the Caribbean. The end result was a relative lack of growth in nightlife entertainment whose prosperity depended largely on tourist dollars.

Nevertheless, Celia Cruz continued to ply her trade in these unfavorable circumstances. She sang whenever and wherever she could, including at balls of the Sociedad Artística Gallega, in small Havana theaters (such as the Cuatro Caminos or the Belascoaín), and at events sponsored by labor organizations.

The inclusion of the Soviet Union in the worldwide alliance against the Nazis would have important political and cultural repercussions in Cuba. The Cuban Communist Party, known as the Partido Socialista Popular (PSP), acquired legal status and, for the first time, was allowed to operate in an open and public manner. The PSP developed a broad cultural agenda that included the acquisition of a radio station, Radio

Lavín, which became Radio Mil Diez because of it location on the dial (1010). Mil Diez featured many popular orchestras and artists. Arcaño y Sus Maravillas, Arsenio Rodríguez, and the Trío Matamoros with Beny Moré were some of the prominent artists whose music was often broadcast live by Mil Diez.

Celia Cruz was joining a very select roster. She sang accompanied by the station's band, conducted by notable Cuban violinist and conductor Enrique González Mantici. The band's rhythm section included the young *bongosero* Ramón "Mongo" Santamaría. Besides Celia, other rising vocalists (including Elena Burke and Olga Guillot) worked at Mil Diez.

With the economic and artistic support of the station, Celia undertook several tours of Cuba. She was usually accompanied by one or two musicians, most often a pianist, who could take charge of the local bands that accompanied Celia. On more than one occasion, the man at the piano was another representative of Cuban music royalty, future mambo king Dámaso Pérez Prado.[8]

In the mid-1940s, Celia Cruz began to work at another Havana radio station, the RHC–Cadena Azul, where she sang accompanied by composer and pianist Isolina Carrillo, author of the memorable bolero "Dos gardenias."[9] It was around this time that one of her aunts, noticing that Celia maintained a rigid stance while singing, suggested she move a bit more while performing. Cruz took the advice to heart, and to the end of her career she complemented her singing with her flashy, rhythmic movements. Celia began to take piano lessons and would eventually complete two years of ear training, solfeggio, and music theory at the Conservatorio Nacional in Havana.

With the end of the war and the subsequent increase in the volume of U.S. tourism, the conditions in the music industry and the opportunities available to musicians began to improve gradually. Nevertheless, Cuba as a whole remained a country condemned to the sugarcane monoculture. This condition was maintained largely because of the economic power of a few U.S.-based companies operating on the island

and because of the overall political domination of Cuban affairs by the United States.

During the sugarcane harvest season, several hundred thousand workers were employed to cut, load, and do other necessary tasks to carry the raw cane stalks to the giant sugar mill processing plants. The extensive nature of sugarcane cultivation in Cuba permitted a very brief harvest season that lasted at the most three months. The remainder of the year, named the *tiempo muerto* (dead time), was witness to the mass unemployment of nearly half a million agricultural workers and peasants. The unemployed roamed the island looking for work or, if lucky, retreated to small sharecropping parcels where they survived on a diet of yams, yucca, and plantains. The majority suffered year round from hunger and health deprivation, either in the countryside or in the marginal barrios of the larger urban centers. This economic structure had produced a steady pattern of permanent migrants to the capital city of Havana who sought a solution to the miserable conditions that prevailed in the rural areas. Many found their escape in the music profession.

Fortunately for humanity, in that "empresa consolidada de la ricura que es Cuba" (that conglomerate enterprise of sweetness which is Cuba),[10] there was an abundance of marvelous musicians full of talent, many barely surviving in the most abject poverty, in search of a chance to make a living performing. These artists, despite hardships, could rely on Cuba's splendid repertoire, the product of more than four centuries of transculturation of European and African traditions. So it came to pass that in a Havana invaded by U.S. tourists looking for tropical pleasures, casinos, and prostitution, Cuban musicians of humble origin developed in the post–World War II years some of the most complex forms of world dance music of the twentieth century. The attentive listener can detect here and there a sentiment of sadness in the music of that era. It should be no surprise that the frustrated dreams of the rural folk manifested themselves through the melancholy minor tones of the popular *guajiras* of the times.

Celia Cruz was only one of many who struggled to advance in the midst of these adverse conditions. In 1946, she accepted an offer to work in a show at Havana's Teatro Fausto. The performance, entitled *Sinfonía en blanco y negro,* was choreographed by Roderico Neyra, with music by Bobby Collazo. Besides Celia, other vocalists included Elena Burke and Xiomara Alfaro. The main feature of the show was the sexy dancing of a group of attractive young women to tunes sung by Celia, which included current hits such as "Puntillita" and "Meneíto pa'ca." The show was a great success. It remained onstage for two years, by the end of which time it had been renamed the *Mulatas de fuego* show.

Celia worked other jobs, primarily live shows in theaters and extravagant events at the famed Havana nightclubs. She was well paid for her singing at the Tropicana, Sans Souci, and Montmartre nightclubs, where she enjoyed the accompaniment of big bands for which Bebo Valdés often wrote the arrangements.[11] It was during this period that Celia Cruz recorded a number of tunes, first with the Conjunto Gloria Matancera and later as vocalist for several *batá*-accompanied Santería songs.

Meanwhile, the popularity of the *Mulatas de fuego* expanded beyond Cuba. In 1948, Celia and the *"mulatas"* traveled abroad for the first time in a lengthy trek that would take them to Mexico and Venezuela. For several years, Cuban musicians had migrated to Mexico City, home of the main recording companies and a thriving night entertainment industry. Some prominent musicians who sought fame and fortune there included Humberto Cané, Miguel Matamoros, Beny Moré, Silvestre Méndez, Juan Bruno Tarraza, Mongo Santamaría, and Armando Peraza. Several famous Cuban *rumberas,* such as María Antonieta Pons, Rosa Carmina, and Ninón Sevilla, had established themselves as the main attraction in a number of lavish shows and also appeared as dancers in many Mexican films of the 1940s. Mexico City's public received Celia and the *mulatas* with open arms when the troupe began their tour at El Zombie cabaret. During this, her first visit to Mexico, Celia met the great vocalist of tropical tunes Toña La Negra as well as many other show business figures.

The Mexico City chapter of the tour lasted three months. The group flew next to Caracas, Venezuela, where they remained two more months. In Caracas, they performed at the renowned Taberna del Silencio. Celia took advantage of the Venezuela trip to record again, this time with the Sonora Caracas, and to travel to the western city of Maracaibo, where she sang with the all-woman Cuban orchestra Anacaona.

THE SONORA MATANCERA

Returning home, Celia went to work for another radio station, Radio Cadena Suaritos, singing in the *coro* (chorus) for the Santería music that came into fashion toward the end of the decade. But she disliked her secondary role. Thus, when she learned that the Sonora Matancera's popular singer Mirta Silva was returning to her native Puerto Rico, Celia sought out the group's contact, Rogelio Martínez. Soon she signed an exclusive contract with the Sonora to perform and record for the Seeco label.

The Sonora Matancera was a seasoned *conjunto* founded in Matanzas by Valentín Cané in 1924 and dedicated to the playing of traditional Cuban *son*. For reasons of health and age, Cané allowed the management of the group to be taken over gradually by the group's guitarist, Rogelio Martínez. Neither a founder nor an exceptional guitarist, Martínez had a knack for maintaining relations and handling the affairs of the Sonora.

While the majority of the Cuban *son conjuntos* from the 1920s and 1930s had either lost popularity or disappeared altogether, the Sonora Matancera carried on, thanks in large measure to a collective and disciplined style of work. Each member of the Sonora was responsible for specific tasks, and the entire organization was run as a cooperative.

This modus operandi, and the development and maintenance of good social and political contacts, allowed the Sonora Matancera to survive the dreadful economic depression of the 1930s and the accompanying difficulties associated with the music business.

In the 1940s, as we have discussed earlier, Cuban popular music underwent a number of significant changes. Arsenio Rodríguez successfully used the conga drum in the *conjunto* format, while Antonio Arcaño and the López brothers (Orestes and Israel "Cachao") began a series of innovations that would eventually lead to the mambo.[12] From a macro view of the development of Cuban popular music, it is probably the case that the Sonora Matancera did not play the more interesting or complex music of the day. It possessed neither the rich syncopations of the Conjunto Arsenio Rodríguez nor the harmonic/rhythmic complexity of the Orquesta de Beny Moré of the 1950s. In terms of popularity, the most sought-out *conjuntos* were others, such as the Conjunto Casino and the Conjunto Kubavana.[13]

Nevertheless, the experienced Sonora Matancera achieved tremendous success accompanying a variety of singers who became popular in quick succession. Most important for the future popularity of the Sonora, many of these vocalists were not themselves Cuban but came from other Latin American countries. Thus, Mirta Silva, Daniel Santos, and Bobby Capó were all Puerto Ricans; Alberto Beltrán hailed from the Dominican Republic; Nelson Pinedo came from Colombia; and Leo Marini and Carlos Argentino were from Argentina. The characteristic *sabor* of Cuban music began to spread throughout Latin America ever more rapidly through the voices of these Latin American singers.

The Sonora Matancera played Cuban music well, neither too fast nor too slow, and always accompanied accomplished vocalists. While a number of Cuban *conjuntos* used the descriptive title "Sonora," such as Sonora Musical, Sonora Nacional, and Sonora de Piñón, it was the Sonora Matancera that became a model to many groups throughout the

Caribbean basin. In Venezuela, Mexico, Colombia, and other countries, musical ensembles took up the name "Sonora" and even attempted to imitate the sound of the Matancera.[14]

Celia's first appearance with the Sonora Martancera took place on August 3, 1950, on a Havana variety radio show sponsored by a laundry soap company. In a short period of time, the program became a national favorite. She also recorded the first tunes under her new contract, "Cao cao, maní picao" and "Mata siguaraya." In the years that followed, Celia continued to sing with the Sonora Matancera on radio and television and became one of the leading figures of Havana's thriving nightlife. She shared the stage with important local figures such as Beny Moré as well as with internationally known performers such as Josephine Baker.

Celia Cruz was featured in many shows at name cabarets such as the Tambú, the Zombie, and the Topeka and at the Encanto and Fausto Theatres. She appeared at the special production *Maracas en la noche* at the Sans Souci nightclub and at the Tropicana, together with singers Merceditas Valdés and Paulina Alvarez in a three-part spectacular entitled *Pregón negro, Danzonete, Bembé santero.* Her voice and image became one of the most successful musical commodities to come out of 1950s Havana. She appeared in a series of movies with the Sonora Matancera,[15] had a part in a popular soap opera, toured the island, and recorded such a large number of jingles—for cigarettes, soaps, soft drinks, cheese, coffee, beer, and so forth—that she came to be called by another "royal" title, Queen of the Jingles.

Although Celia was already known outside of Cuba, her years with the Sonora Matancera catapulted her fame to new heights. With the Sonora, she traveled to Haiti in 1952 and then took a solo trip to Colombia in 1953. A few months before this trip, Celia met one of her idols, Colombian vocalist Matilde Díaz, who was visiting Havana with her husband, the noted Colombian composer Lucho Bermúdez. This was the beginning of a friendship that lasted throughout Celia's life.[16] During her first visit to Colombia, Celia appeared in Cartagena, where she sang at the Hotel Caribe, and also in Bogotá and Medellín. In subsequent years, she traveled with the Sonora Matancera to Panama, Costa Rica, and Colombia (several times) as well as Nicaragua, Curaçao, and Venezuela. Celia visited New York for the first time in 1957 to receive an award for her first "gold" tune, "Burundanga." She traveled on her own to Puerto Rico in 1958, where the orchestra of César Concepción provided accompaniment. In Puerto Rico, she shared the stage at the Flamboyán Cabaret with Cortijo y Su Combo and Ismael Rivera.

From Puerto Rico, Celia traveled directly to Los Angeles, California, where she appeared at the Million Dollar Theatre and at the Hollywood Palladium. Her local backup orchestra in Los Angeles included the veteran Cuban flutist Rolando Lozano, of early Orquesta Aragón fame.

In a short span of time, six years at the most, Celia Cruz and the Sonora Matancera recorded a long list of tunes that would become classics of Cuban music and, later, salsa. Here are some of them: "Agua pa' mí," "Burundanga," "Abre la puerta querida," "Bajo la luna," "Caramelo," "Yerbero moderno," "Mi soncito," "Nuevo ritmo omelenko," "Yembe laroco," "Bemba colorá," "Sopa en botella," "Pinar del Río," and "Ritmo, tambor y flores." In addition to her contract with the Sonora, Celia was free to appear with a wide variety of groups, in and out of Cuba, as well as on radio and television. In her Havana nightclub engagements, she was accompanied by large show orchestras, such as the Orquesta Riverside, but also by small trios for special occasions.

Celia Cruz was never merely a vocalist with a great voice who happened to record a large number of hit tunes. She personally selected each of the songs that became successful commercially, often against the advice of composers and promoters who wanted her to record something else. Celia studied the lyrics and music of tunes brought to her attention, sang them to herself, and decided which to record as well as which to discard. But her involvement did not stop there. She worried about the danger of monotony arising from the similarity of arrangements. Although while working with the Sonora she relied mainly on the group's arranger, Severino Ramos, but also sought arrangements from other musicians such as Niño Rivera and Roberto Puente. In the LPs from her Sonora Matancera years, Celia normally utilized three or four different arrangers, an attention to detail that kept her material from sounding repetitive. Thus, her success was founded not only on her stage and vocal qualities but also on her steady and methodical handling of the whole of her artistic projects.

Therein lies the importance of the role played by Celia Cruz in the diffusion and popularity of Cuban music. Those carefully selected *sones* and *guarachas* she sang became so popular throughout the Caribbean basin that they eventually became part of the cultural heritage, not just of Cuba but of the entire region. One example alone attests to her influence in the Caribbean music of the 1950s: between 1955 and 1958, Celia Cruz and the Sonora Matancera were featured for four consecutive years at the Venezuela carnivals in Caracas. The Sonora, of course, was not alone: in 1958, more than twenty Cuban music groups participated in the Venezuela carnivals, but the distinct sound of Celia and the Sonora stood out as in previous years.

Many Latin Americans who grew up in the Caribbean with the familiar sound of Celia Cruz's voice would migrate in later years to urban centers in the United States. New York, Chicago, Los Angeles, San Francisco, and other cities became centers of attraction for immigrants fleeing the lack of employment and opportunities in their home countries. In the decade of the 1970s, this growing mass of Latinos became an immediate consumer market for a new musical synthesis, a new salsa. For all of these Latinos, whether they were from Colombia, Venezuela, Panama, the Dominican Republic, or elsewhere, this salsa was something of their own, a sound they identified as part of their homegrown cultural heritage.

Many of those who as children enjoyed the voice of Celia and the Sonora Matancera's trumpeters, Calixto Leicea and Pedrito Knight, would develop into fans, and even practitioners, of Latin jazz, perhaps the most exciting contemporary urban sound.

LEAVING CUBA BEHIND

The revolution of 1959 drastically changed the structure of Cuban society. The music industry was no exception. The decline in the flow of United States tourism to the island and the eventual break of diplomatic relations with the United States brought down the entire economic scaffolding that supported the tourist industry and, by extension, much of the music business in Havana.

Many distinguished musicians remained in Cuba, but many left for other countries. Celia Cruz and the Sonora Matancera left for Mexico in July 1960 for a brief tour and did not return to Cuba. The Mexico tour began on July 15 with a performance at the Teatro Lírico in Mexico City; one week later, Celia appeared with a refurbished *Mulatas de fuego* troupe at the Terraza Casino Club in the same city. She was to remain in Mexico for a year and a half. During that period, she joined Toña la Negra for a countrywide tour and appeared in the movie *Amorcito corazón,* in which she sang the memorable bolero "Tu voz." But she felt constrained by the limitations of the Mexican tropical music market. So in 1962, she did not renew her contract with the Sonora Matancera and Seeco records.

Despite the pleas of her friend and noted Mexican composer Agustín Lara, Celia decided to try her luck in the United States, where she married trumpeter Pedro Knight on July 14, 1962. The ensuing decade represents the low point in Celia's career. The large recording labels were not interested in promoting a "Cuban music" product at a time of missile crises and invasions. She appeared in various cities in the United States but kept returning to Mexico for engagements in Mexico City and Acapulco. In 1965, she rejoined the Sonora Matancera briefly for a trip to Venezuela, but otherwise the decade remained void of the great success and economic promise that the 1950s had held for her.

TITO PUENTE

The Cuban exiles who settled in Miami after the 1959 revolution in Cuba belonged for the most part to the well-to-do sector and professional elites of the country. Their economic and political worries left little time or interest for promoting the island's powerful Afro-Cuban music. Miami was the principal city in Florida, a region with more than its share of antiblack racial prejudice. Thus, it should come as no surprise that neither Celia Cruz nor many other Cuban musicians chose to stay in Miami to ply their musical trade.

But New York was different. For several decades, Cuban artists had been turning the Big Apple into an artistic mecca. Among the many Cuban artists and musicians who had come to live and work in New York since the 1930s were Alberto Socarrás, Mario Bauzá, Machito, Miguelito Valdés, Chano Pozo, Mongo Santamaría, Patato Valdés, Graciela Grillo, Luis Carbonell, Chocolate Armenteros, Vicentico Valdés, and Panchito Riset. Cuban and Puerto Rican musicians formed the core of numerous musical groups that played dance music for the Spanish-speaking community of the city and surrounding areas.

There was in New York a large settlement of Spanish-speaking musicians, mostly of Puerto Rican origin, who had adopted and transformed Cuban music, treating it with "more care and respect than Cubans themselves."[17] One of those Puerto Rican musicians, Ernesto "Tito" Puente, extended Celia a helping hand in her moment of need. Beginning in late 1966, they began to work under contract with the Tico label. Over the next seven years, Tito and Celia would release eight LPs: *Celia y Tito, Quimbo quimbumbia, Etc-etc, Algo especial, Alma con alma, En España,* and a collection of greatest hits. At the same time, by special arrangement with Tico Records, Celia Cruz recorded an LP with the orchestra of Memo Salamanca in Mexico.

With these orchestras, Celia returned to the kind of accompaniment she had enjoyed in Havana nightclubs: large bands of fourteen or more musicians, twice the size of the Sonora Matancera. Yet the recordings met with little success. Perhaps the public was not accustomed to the new sound behind Celia's voice or promotion was not up to the circumstances. Perhaps it was simply that public tastes had changed: after all, the tearful sound of La Lupe, quite different from Celia's, was the rage in New York at the time. None of the recordings produced memorable results. In those eight LPs Celia Cruz tried everything: she flirted with the *bugalú* and even tried *ranchera a go go* in the recordings with Memo Salamanca. Perhaps the only tune that received grudging acceptance from the public was Tito and Celia's version of "Aquarius." During this period with Tito Puente, Celia divided her time between New York and Mexico City, where she and Pedro kept an apartment. With Tito Puente, Celia Cruz traveled again to Venezuela and joined the Sonora Matancera for brief appearances.

PACHECO AND WILLIE COLÓN

In the early 1970s, events took a turn for the better. First, pianist Larry Harlow invited Celia to record the music for his Latin music opera *Hommy*.[18] While the recording still did not score high points with the public, it signaled the beginning of a relationship with the new Fania label. Fania would soon place Celia Cruz at the vanguard of a salsa recording boom that would last the next fifteen years.

So it was that in 1974, Celia met up with a Dominican musician of prominent merengue ancestry, flutist Johnny Pacheco.[19] Their first recording for Fania, the LP *Celia y Johnny,* was a blockbuster. It included an interesting combination of old and new tunes; some was Cuban material and the rest was from other Latin American countries. Among the old tunes, Celia selected Orlando de la Rosa's "Vieja luna." She had to do battle with Fania executives, who did not wish to include Junior Cepeda's "Quimbara." Celia won the battle, and "Quimbara" went on to become her theme song in all of her Fania All-Stars concerts.

As in previous eras, the key to this great success was Celia's uncanny ability to choose material for recordings. Another song that she selected for the LP, "Toro mata," from Afro-Peruvian folklore, also became a memorable hit. Two more LPs of Celia and Pacheco appeared in quick order. *Tremendo caché* was released in 1975. It contained an old favorite from the 1950s Sonora Matancera days, "Sopita en botella," and a salsa version of Ismael Rivera's *bomba* "Cúcala." The third LP in the series, *Recordando el ayer,* appealed to nostalgia as a marketing tool. It included a number of standard old hits such as "Besitos de coco," "Ritmo, tambor y flores," and "Yerbero moderno."

Celia Cruz had always been a fan of the popular music of all of Latin America. In particular she revered the folklore of Venezuela and Peru and the compositions of Colombian Lucho Bermúdez. She loved to sing Mexican *rancheras.* This Latin American bent became obvious in her next Fania recording with Willie Colón, released in 1977, in which she used a song from Brazil, "Usted abusó"; a *bomba* from Puerto Rico, "A papá"; a Dominican merengue, "Pun, pun, catalú"; a salsified *ranchera,* "Tú y las nubes"; her Cuban standard "Burundanga"; and an Uruguayan tune with a Panamanian-rhythm arrangement, "Zambúllete y ven pa' cá." After the successful collaboration with Willie Colón, Celia released yet another LP with Johnny Pacheco, *Eternos,* in 1978. On it she included old themes such as "El cocoyé" and "Yembé laroco" as well as new tunes, such as the merengue "El guabá." Celia's next release was with Fania artist Papo Lucca and his Sonora Ponceña *conjunto.* Their joint LP, *La ceiba y la siguaraya,* was another great success. Once again, she chose a Latin American mixture: Cuban standards such as "Sonaremos el tambor," the Puerto Rican *bomba* "A la buena sí," and one of her favorite songs from Peruvian Chabuca Granda's repertoire, "Fina estampa."

Throughout this period, Celia's affinity for Latin American music helped transform and enrich her older Cuban songbook, adding new elements, rhythms, and tinges to her *sones* and *guarachas* and leading to the peak of salsa. This synthesis became a new concept that belonged to all of Latin America. With the Fania All-Stars, Celia Cruz traveled throughout Latin America, visiting Colombia and Peru several times as well as Puerto Rico, Venezuela, the Dominican Republic, and other countries. She also went to the heart of Africa as part of the musical extravaganza that surrounded the legendary "rumble in the jungle" between Muhammad Ali and George Foreman for the heavyweight boxing championship.

Audiences worldwide began to identify Celia Cruz in part through her striking performance outfits. In that aspect, too, Celia exercised direct care over the smallest details. For each public performance she chose the fabric and color she would wear. For many years a few select tailors, with whom she worked closely, would sew her clothes. The management of her physical persona extended literally from head to foot. Thus she often wore high shoes without pointy heels, specially made for her by a Mexican shoemaker, which avoided the danger of a thin high heel getting stuck in a crevice on the stage and causing her to trip.

Celia's success continued unabated in the 1980s. Fania released a second LP with Celia and Willie Colón in 1981, which contained the catchy tunes "Cucurrucucú paloma," "Los dos jueyes," and "Apaga la luz." In quick order, Celia recorded LPs with the Sonora Matancera (1982), Ray Barretto (1983), Tito Puente (*Homenaje a Beny Moré,* 1985), and Ray Barreto again (1988), for which she received a Grammy Award. In that decade, Celia Cruz arrived at the pinnacle of her fame. She appeared in every country of Latin America, with the exception of Bolivia and Paraguay, and in every major city in the United States. Celia performed live in France, in Japan with Tito Puente, and in Switzerland, Germany, Greece, and Italy. She sang in a duo with noted flamenco artist Lola Flores in Spain and appeared in Portugal, England, and Finland. In an indefatigable streak, she performed on the widest variety of stages: from Carnegie Hall in Manhattan to an open-air stage in Esmeraldas, Ecuador, under a torrential downpour. On the latter occasion she slipped and fell, breaking a leg. Two days later she was back onstage in the Dominican Republic, the leg in a cast disguised by lamé boots. She recorded *rock en español* with the Argentine group Fabulosos Cadillacs, joined rock star David Byrne for a collaborative project, and became a character in Latin American literature in the *Reina rumba* of Colombia's Umberto Valverde.

CELIA OF THE AMERICAS

In the years before the new millennium, Celia Cruz received more than one hundred prizes and awards, including the keys to the cities of Lima, Paris, and New York. Twenty of her LPs had reached the gold category by then. She had received three Grammys and been nominated for more than twelve. She was awarded two honorary degrees, from Yale and from Florida International University. Hollywood granted her a star on its Walk of Fame. She appeared in several movies, including *The Mambo Kings* and *The Perez Family;* worked on several Mexican TV soap operas; and was the subject of a PBS television special in late 1999.[20] Her tours of the world continued nonstop, from Peru to Spain and from Hollywood to Rio de Janeiro, where she sang with Caetano Veloso. In 1993, Celia was present at the fiftieth anniversary of Colombia's Matilde Díaz's artistic career—they both sang "Burundanga" for the occasion.[21]

In the early 1990s, she also signed a contract with Ralph Mercado and his RMM records and released two more successful CDs: *Azúcar negra* and *Irrepetible.* For the latter, Celia insisted on the inclusion of a tune that turned out to be the number-one hit in the entire recording, "Que le den candela." For RMM she also sang a theme for a special recording in tribute to the Beatles.[22] In 2002, she released her CD *La negra tiene tumbao,* in which she connected with the world of hip-hop and rap music. She continued to record even after she had been operated on for a brain tumor and told that her days were numbered.

In his book on Cuban music, Cristóbal Díaz Ayala underlines the importance of salsa as an amalgam of rhythms that served to build bridges among the various Latino communities in the United States. As discussed earlier, it worked, according to the same author, as a form of cultural defense in the Caribbean basin against the dominant and diluting tendencies of the easy pop and rock musics originating in the United States.[23] In my estimation, salsa indeed provided the feeling of a common cultural bond not only in the United States but also throughout many Latin American countries. Salsa was a musical concept developed by Latin Americans for Latin Americans, regardless of place of birth or residence.

The role of Celia Cruz was essential to this process. Twice in the course of a career that spanned more than six decades, Celia used her music to draw together Latin American cultural strands. In the 1950s, the sound of her voice and the instruments of the Sonora Matancera caused a "Matancerization" of the entire Caribbean basin. And in the 1970s, she became the ambassador of Latin American salsa around the world. Her voice, music, and songs represent a significant chapter in the cultural history of Latin America, a history that developed distinct from the Anglophone music world and often in opposition to it.

As I have noted before, this important development did not occur fortuitously. In Celia's brilliant period with the Sonora Matancera, the popularity of the group's music was due in large part to Celia's meticulous choice of songs and arrangers as well as to the discipline and talent with which she managed every aspect of performance and recording. In the 1970s, Celia stuck to her style of artistic work. She also used her personal influence to add her passion for Latin American folklore and traditions to the Caribbean core of the music. Thus, the feeling of unity that arose among Latin Americans around salsa music is not a mere coincidence: it was partly the consequence of the direct artistic intervention of Celia Cruz, who, for instance, transformed "Fina estampa" from a Peruvian into a Latin American classic and made "A papá" much more than another hit by Mon Rivera.

Celia Cruz was known strictly as a Cuban music and salsa vocalist, with little standing in the world of jazz, or, for that matter, Latin jazz.

Upon reflection, however, the growth of Latin jazz in South America was made easier after Cuban dance music had taken root in many countries in the area and local musicians had absorbed its rhythmic elements. Throughout the twentieth century, varieties of Cuban music tended to spread in different directions. And while the styles of Machito and Arsenio Rodríguez found a home in the United States, the more laid-back, less syncopated sounds of Celia Cruz and her backup band, the Sonora Matancera, were adopted from Mexico to all points south. Celia Cruz thus played an important, although perhaps unwitting, role in connecting Afro-Cuban rhythms to Latin jazz. She contributed decisively in laying the foundation that allowed generations of younger musicians to experiment and develop new avenues for this music of the Americas.

Thanks largely to her own initiative, Celia Cruz altered the character of the music she recorded until it became part of the living folklore of the Americas. The Queen of Salsa and Rumba, the Guarachera of Cuba and Oriente, she was an honored musical citizen of all of the Americas.[24] Through talent and dedication, she propelled the sound of Afro-Caribbean dance music—the foundation of Latin jazz—to the world stage.

AFTERWORD

I have focused on popular dance rhythms in the foregoing chapters, as they are nationally and internationally the most widely known, and the most influential, aspects of Cuban music. But Cuban music is a vast and varied subject. The preceding analyses are but a first step in the task of exploring, analyzing, explaining, and enjoying it.

A second step would be to develop and tie together a number of strands that have been merely hinted at in this book. For example, Cuban music has a strong instrumental tradition of forms designed not only for dancing but also for listening and meditative enjoyment. Aside from the chapter on Cachao and the related *descarga* music, this book does not treat instrumental music extensively. Since the 1940s in partic-ular, a tradition of Cuban popular instrumental music established itself in the national music panorama. Some of these developments are closely connected with the growth of jazz in Cuba; sometimes the line between Cuban popular instrumental music and Latin jazz is quite blurred.

Focusing on instrumental music brings to the fore another issue, namely the characteristics and evolution of styles of improvisation within Cuban popular genres. Most of the individuals connected with these aspects of Cuban music carried out their work, for the most part, in Cuba itself. A list of such musicians would be very long, but a few who deserve mention are Bebo Valdés, Frank Emilio Flynn, Richard Egües, Chucho Valdés, and Tata Güines.

Within a study of popular dance influences on Cuban music, another necessary step would be to look in some detail at other building blocks besides the *son,* such as the rumba, the *danzón,* the *música guajira,* and the *canción* tradition. The evolution of Cuban popular music in the twentieth century and today has been characterized by a constant mixing and remixing, twisting and turning, of all of these local genres. Some musicians worth mentioning in this regard are Sindo Garay, Ignacio Piñeiro, and César Portillo de la Luz. Finally, if the story of Cuban popular music begins, as we detailed, with the transformation of the French *contredanse* into the Cuban *contradanza,* and later the habanera, the *danzón,* and so on, this is a process that we see repeated throughout the twentieth century and even today, as Cuban musicians have synthesized American rap with Cuban genres to produce something unique that they call, for lack of a better name, Cuban rap. Cuban musicians introduced multiple expressions of world music—in the most generic sense of that term— into their dance compositions throughout the last century and continue to do so. My good friend Carlos del Puerto—for twenty-five years the bassist of Irakere—commented to me once that Cuban people had gotten to know Mozart, Verdi, Tchaikovsky, Broadway musicals, Spanish *zarzuelas,* Italian melodies, Argentine tangos, the blues, and so forth simply by dancing to the hundreds of *danzones* that utilized and sometimes modified themes and melodies from all those varied sources.

There is clearly much more that needs to be studied about Cuban music. *¡Qué no se pare la rumba!*

NOTES

Preface

1. The rhumba was actually an orchestral version of the Cuban dance, the *son,* which was already popular in the Caribbean. *Rhumba,* spelled with an "h," is used in this book to distinguish it from a different, drum-based, folkloric dance known in Cuba as the *rumba,* although the two spellings have been used interchangeably in the United States.

2. Howard Reich, "Orquesta Aragón Alters Perception of Afro-Cuban Jazz," *Chicago Tribune,* June 15, 2000.

PART I

1. There have been many attempts to conceptualize the unity of the Caribbean. See, for example, Ileana Rodríguez and Marc Zimmerman, eds., *Process of Unity in Caribbean Society: Ideologies and Literature* (Minneapolis: Institute for the Study of Ideologics and Literature, 1983); Antonio Benítez Rojo, *The Repeating Island* (Durham, NC: Duke University Press, 1982). See also the very ambitious effort by Samuel Floyd Jr., "Black Music in the Circum-Caribbean," *American Music* 17 (Spring 1999): 1–37.

2. This brief account of Gottschalk's musical activities is taken from Fred-

erick Starr, *Bamboula! The Life and Times of Louis Moreau Gottschalk* (New York: Oxford University Press, 1995).

3. *Contradanza:* a nineteenth-century Cuban ballroom dance derived from the English country dance and the courtly French *contredanse* and Spanish *contradanza*. It led to the very similar pan-Caribbean *danza*. Tango: a syncopated ostinato beat also known as the habanera beat. *Cinquillo:* a five-beat rhythmic pattern characteristic of the *contradanza* and many other Cuban and Caribbean genres.

4. Rudolf Frederik Willem Boskaljon, *Honderd jaar muziekleven op Curaçao* (Assen, The Netherlands, 1958), cited in Robert Stevenson, *A Guide to Caribbean Music History* (Lima: Ediciones Cultura, 1975), 8.

5. On the history of the Palenque de San Basilio, see Aquiles Escalante, *El Palenque de San Basilio* (Barranquilla: Editorial Mejoras, 1979); William W. Megenney, *El palenquero: Un lenguaje post-criollo de Colombia* (Bogotá: Instituto Caro y Cuervo, 1986).

6. Fabio Betancur Alvarez, *Sin clave y bongó no hay son* (Medellín: Editorial Universidad de Antioquia, 1993).

7. Jorge Duany, "Popular Music in Puerto Rico: Toward an Anthropology of Salsa," *Latin American Music Review* 5, no. 2 (1984): 186–216. The *cinquillo* pattern can be heard in other musics of the Francophone Caribbean, for example, the *gwoka* of Guadeloupe and the *bèlè* of Martinique.

8. That all national music forms in the Caribbean contain "international" elements has been noted before. See, for example, Juan Flores, "Bumbum and the Beginning of La Plena," *CENTRO Bulletin* 2 (Spring 1988).

9. *Danzón:* a Cuban musical and dance form developed in the late nineteenth century from the *contradanza* and the *danza;* it is both longer and slower than its predecessors.

10. *Danzón,* a film by María Novaro, Macondo Cine-Video, 1991.

11. Danilo Lozano, "The *Charanga* Tradition in Cuba: History, Style, and Ideology" (master's thesis, Department of Music, UCLA, 1990).

12. Jorge Castellanos and Isabel Castellanos, *Cultura afrocubana* (Miami: Ediciones Universal, 1994), 4:335–40.

13. Starr, *Bamboula!,* 184.

14. The *danzón* also established a unique, very personal connection to the development of jazz. Mario Bauzá, who first came to New York to record *danzones* as the clarinetist for the prominent *charanga* of Antonio María Romeu, returned to settle there in 1930, inspired by the city's vibrant jazz scene. He

would later become the musical director of Machito's Afro-Cuban orchestra and is recognized as the key figure in the development of Afro-Cuban jazz in the 1940s—or Latin jazz, as it is now known.

15. The number of migration flows across linguistic areas in the Caribbean is not insignificant. A few of them have merited the attention of social scientists. See Rosemary Brana-Shute, ed., *A Bibliography of Caribbean Migration and Caribbean Immigrant Communities* (Gainesville: Center for Latin American Studies, University of Florida, 1983).

16. Cited in Peter Manuel, *Caribbean Currents* (Philadelphia: Temple University Press, 1995), 153.

17. Ibid., 154.

18. Fernando Ortiz, *Los instrumentos de la música afrocubana* (Havana: Cárdenas y Cía, 1955), 4:350; also, José Millet and Rafael Brea, *Grupos folklóricos de Santiago de Cuba* (Santiago de Cuba: Editorial Oriente, 1989), 157.

19. Benítez Rojo, *Island.*

20. Personal observation of the author.

21. Notable among these are the Curaçao Salsa Festival and the Caribbean Music Festival of Cartagena, Colombia.

Chapter One

1. For a good history of the stages of Latin dance music in the United States, see John Storm Roberts, *The Latin Tinge* (New York: Oxford University Press, 1979).

2. For a discussion on this point, see, among others, Roberts, *The Latin Tinge,* chap. 8; Charley Gerard (with Marty Sheller), *Salsa!* (Crown Point, IN: White Cliffs Media Company, 1989); and Lise Waxer, ed., *Situating Salsa: Global Markets and Local Meaning in Latin Popular Music* (New York and London: Routledge, 2002).

3. Frances R. Aparicio, *Listening to Salsa: Gender, Latin Popular Music, and Puerto Rican Cultures* (Hanover, NH, and London: Wesleyan University Press, 1998).

4. Richard J. Cadena, "Mexico: Los años cuarenta y cincuenta," *Latin Beat,* November 1992, 15.

5. Steven Loza, *Barrio Rhythm: Mexican-American Music in Los Angeles* (Chicago: University of Illinois Press, 1993).

6. Cristóbal Díaz Ayala, *Música cubana: Del areíto a la nueva trova* (San Juan, Puerto Rico: Cubanacán, 1981).

7. Deborah Pacini, "Social Identity and Class in *Bachata*, an Emerging Dominican Popular Music," mimeo, Cornell University, September 1988, p. 3.

8. This phrase is Lise Waxer's. See her *Situating Salsa*, 14.

Chapter Two

1. The Trío Matamoros of the 1920s enjoyed a reputation for playing the most traditional form of *son*—the *son oriental* of Oriente province at the eastern end of Cuba. The percussive *tumbao* of Rafael Cueto was one of its most distinctive characteristics. But Cueto himself stated that he developed the style of adding a slap to the body of the guitar after watching Havana bassist Ignacio Piñeiro striking the body of his bass during live performances in the 1920s. See Hernán Restrepo Duque, *Lo que cuentan los boleros* (Bogotá: Centro Editorial de Estudios Musicales, 1992), 182.

2. I am indebted for this observation to Radamés Giro.

3. On Spanish music, please see Gilbert Chase, *The Music of Spain* (New York: W. W. Norton, 1941).

4. On the ethnic origins of Cubans of African descent, please see Jorge Castellanos and Isabel Castellanos, "The Geographic, Ethnologic and Linguistic Roots of Cuban Blacks," *Cuban Studies* 17 (1987): 95–110.

5. The interested reader may wish to consult Fernando Ortiz, *Los instrumentos de la música afrocubana*, 5 vols. (Havana: Ministerio de Educación, 1952), for an exhaustive catalog of drums of African pedigree. A more recent reference work on the same subject is Victoria Eli Rodriguez and others, *Instrumentos de la música folclórico popular de Cuba* (Havana: Editorial de Ciencias Sociales, 1997).

6. I am grateful to Carlos del Puerto for this wording.

7. Puerto Rican poet Víctor Hernández Cruz offers this captivating description of Afro-Caribbean salsa dancing in *Red Beans* (Minneapolis: Coffee House Press, 1991), 97.

8. I am indebted to Katherine Hagedorn for helping me through the analysis of *tres* playing styles.

9. Luis Tamargo, "Paquito D'Rivera," *Latin Beat*, April 1992, 22.

10. See Rebeca Mauleón, *101 Montunos* (Petaluma, CA: Sher Music, 1999).

11. On the controversy surrounding the origins of the *son*, see Alejo Car-

pentier, *La música en Cuba* (Havana: Editorial Luz-Hilo, 1961); Alberto Muguercia, "Teodora Ginés: Mito o realidad histórica?" *Revista de la Biblioteca Nacional José Martí,* (September–December 1971); and Argeliers León, *Del canto y el tiempo* (Havana: Editorial Pueblo y Educación, 1974).

12. See n. 11.

13. The great *sonero* and *tresero* Humberto Cané (1918–2000) recalled how his grandfather, father of Sonora Matancera founder Valentín Cané, migrated from Santiago to Matanzas in the last part of the nineteenth century. According to Humberto Cané, his grandfather brought to Matanzas for the first time the small timbales named *timbalitos* particular to Santiago de Cuba. These *timbalitos* were, for a long time, one of the distinguishing characteristics of the Sonora Matancera sound. Personal communication with the author, September 1999.

14. See Jorge Castellanos and Isabel Castellanos, *Cultura afrocubana* (Miami: Ediciones Universal, 1990), 2:247.

15. See Danilo Orozco, notes to his LP *Antología integral del son,* LD-286, EGREM, 1988.

16. The political significance of popular Cuban dance styles is analyzed by John Chasteen's "A National Rhythm: Social Dance and Elite Identity in Nineteenth Century Havana," mimeo, University of North Carolina, Chapel Hill, 2000.

17. The *décima* is named *espinela* after its creator, seventeenth-century Spanish poet Vicente Espinel. He is also remembered for adding a fifth string, or *bordón,* to the traditional Spanish four-string guitar, testimony to the ancient connection between Spanish poetry and popular guitar forms.

18. Merry Mac Masters describes a legendary improvised controversy between Beny Moré and Cheo Marquetti that took place in Mexico City in the late 1940s in her book *Recuerdos del son* (Mexico City: Consejo Nacional para la Cultura y las Artes, 1995).

19. See Nicolás Guillén, *Motivos de son: Edición especial 50 aniversario* (Havana: Editorial Letras Cubanas, 1980); *El son entero: Cantos para soldados y sones para turistas,* 5th ed. (Buenos Aires: Losada, 1971); *Sóngoro cosongo: Poemas mulatos* (Mexico City: Presencia Latinoamericana, 1981).

20. Leonardo Padura Fuentes, *Los rostros de la salsa* (Havana: Ediciones Unión, 1997), 41.

21. Danilo Lozano, in liner notes to his CD *Cuba L.A.,* Narada Productions, 1998.

Chapter Three

1. The translations provided in parentheses are literal ones; they do not capture the idiomatic nuances typical of Cuban Spanish. This chapter was conceived as a performance itself. The use of the language reflects the colloquialisms in song titles and lyrics. Cuban music has developed its own particular vocabulary. Talking about Cuban music without employing it is like talking about jazz without mentioning swing or analyzing Western art music without using terms such as allegro, legato, fortissimo, and so forth.

2. Armando Peraza, conversation with the author, June 1998.

3. The history of these migrations is found in a variety of seminal texts on Cuban music. See, for example, Argeliers León, *Música folklórica cubana* (Havana: Biblioteca Nacional José Martí, 1964); Cristóbal Díaz Ayala, *Música cubana: Del areíto a la nueva trova* (San Juan, Puerto Rico: Cubanacán, 1981).

4. Helio Orovio, *Diccionario de la música cubana* (Havana: Editorial Letras Cubanas, 1992), 303.

5. Don Heckman, "Feeling the Heat with Los Van Van," *Los Angeles Times,* June 16, 1997, sec. E.

6. A *sonero* must be able to improvise lyrics in a manner that fits rhythmically and melodically with the accompanying *coro* of the *montuno.*

7. Israel "Cachao" López, interview by the author for Smithsonian Institution Jazz Oral History Program, January 24–25, 1995, in Miami.

8. A brief glossary of technical terms in Cuban music should also include *tumbao, martillo, guajeo, tresillo, descarga, montuno, capetillo, diana, meta, abanico, caballo, ponche, bombo,* mambo, *tapao, machete,* and *baqueteo.*

9. Danilo Lozano, "The *Charanga* Tradition in Cuba: History, Style and Ideology" (master's thesis, Department of Music, UCLA, 1990).

10. Yvonne Daniel, *Rumba: Dance and Social Change in Contemporary Cuba* (Bloomington: Indiana University Press, 1995).

11. Emilio Grenet, *Popular Cuban Music* (Havana: Ministerio de Educación, 1939).

12. Mayra A. Martínez, *Cubanos en la música* (Havana: Editorial Letras Cubanas, 1993), 333.

13. Rapper John, conversation in a street in Havana with the author, August 12, 2003.

14. This poetic image based on a Cuban colloquialism might be translated as being "powerful in the pussy." I am grateful to Nivia Montenegro for mentioning to me this usage by Oliva.

15. Raul Fernandez, "The Course of U.S. Cuban Music: Margin and Mainstream," *Cuban Studies* 24 (December 1994): 118.

16. Ibid., 116–18.

17. Some prominent names of these family lineages are Egües, Lozano, Hierrezuelo, Formell, Montecinos, Vivar, Escalante, Armenteros, Grillo, de los Reyes, Lecuona, Márquez, Cané, Urfé, Belén Puig, Oviedo, Rubalcaba, Jústiz, Romeu, Chappottín, Ruiz, Abreu, Puerto, Hernández, and Valera-Miranda.

18. Jesús Gómez Cairo, coordinator, *El arte musical de Ernesto Lecuona* (Madrid: Sociedad General de Autores y Editores, 1995), 243.

19. Radamés Giro, Introducción to *Panorama de la música popular cubana,* ed. Radamés Giro (Havana: Editorial Letras Cubanas, 1996), 9.

PART II

1. Much of the material contained in these essays was developed as part of my work as a consultant for the Smithsonian Institution Jazz Oral History Program (JOHP). From 1994 to 2000, I researched the musical biographies of a number of prominent musicians in the fields of Cuban music and Latin jazz. I also conducted detailed interviews with them in Los Angeles, San Francisco, New York, Miami, Havana, Santiago de Cuba, and Stockholm, and I assisted in the preparation of interviews conducted by other JOHP consultants. For these six years I was directly or indirectly involved in background research and interviews with Israel "Cachao" López, Armando Peraza, Mongo Santamaría, Celia Cruz, Chocolate Armenteros, Carlos "Patato" Valdés, Cándido Camero, Arturo "Chico" O'Farrill, Francisco Aguabella, Frank Emilio Flynn, Chucho Valdés, Bebo Valdés, Richard Egües, Luis Carbonell, Celina González, Rodulfo Vaillant, Enrique Bonne, and Antonio "Musiquita" Sánchez.

2. See, for example, Raúl Martínez Rodríguez, *Ellos hacen la música cubana* (Havana: Editorial Letras Cubanas, 1998); John Storm Roberts, *Latin Jazz: The First of the Fusions, 1880s to Today* (New York: Schirmer Books, 1999).

3. Raúl Fernández, *Latin Jazz: The Perfect Combination* (San Francisco: Chronicle Books, 2002); Leonardo Acosta, *Cubano Be, Cubano Bop: One Hundred Years of Jazz in Cuba* (Washington, D.C., Smithsonian Books, 2003); and papers by Max Salazar and Cristóbal Díaz Ayala, presented at the Smithsonian Institution Symposium on Mambo and Afro-Cuban Jazz, February 27, 1999.

Chapter Four

1. Cachao was also the subject of an extensive interview I conducted with Anthony Brown as part of the Smithsonian Institution's Jazz Oral History Program (JOHP). The interview, conducted on January 24–25, 1995, in Miami, provides the basis for some of the analysis and information contained in this chapter.

2. José de Córdoba, "Cuban Musical Legend Gets His Due," *Wall Street Journal,* August 26, 1992.

3. Max Salazar, "The Cubop Story," *Latin Beat,* March 1995.

4. John Storm Roberts, *The Latin Tinge* (New York: Oxford University Press, 1979).

5. For a detailed account, see Jorge Castellanos and Isabel Castellanos, *Cultura afrocubana* (Miami: Ediciones Universal, 1994), 4:341–42.

6. On the origins of the Argentine tango, see Vicente Rossi, *Cosas de negros: Los orígenes del tango y otros aportes al folklore Rioplatense. Rectificaciones históricas* (Córdoba, Argentina: Editorial Imprenta Argentina, 1926).

7. Richard Jackson and Neil Ratliff, *The Little Book of Louis Moreau Gottschalk* (New York: New York Public Library and Continuo Music Press, 1976); see also Ernest Borneman, "Creole Echoes," *Jazz Review* 2 (1959), and Martin Williams, *Jazz Masters of New Orleans* (New York: MacMillan, 1967).

8. Phil Pastras, *Dead Man Blues: Jelly Roll Morton Way Out West* (Berkeley: University of California Press, 2001).

9. Miguel Faílde, a Cuban bandleader steeped in Afro-Cuban religious traditions, is usually credited with the creation of the *danzón.* On the invention and early history of the *danzón* and the role played by Cuban composer Manuel Saumell and Miguel Faílde, the best source still is Alejo Carpentier, *La música en Cuba* (Havana: Editorial Luz-Hilo, 1961).

10. Enrique Romero, "Cachao: Montuno con tradición," *El Manisero* 5 (January–February 1995): 17–21. The *danzonete* is a modified *danzón* characterized by a faster tempo and a larger section for a vocalist. Helio Orovio, *Diccionario de la música cubana* (Havana: Editorial Letras Cubanas, 1992), 141.

11. Cachao's nephew Orlando "Cachaíto" López is also a formidable bassist who played with leading dance orchestras in the 1960s and 1970s. Cachaíto is also among Cuba's leading jazz musicians. He participated in the popular Buena Vista Social Club recordings of the late 1990s.

12. The format of the *danzón,* similar as it was to a rondo (A–B–A–C–A), allowed the introduction of a variety of melodies in popular compositions.

From the turn of the century on, Cuban *danzón* bandleaders would borrow tunes from Mozart, Rossini operas, ragtime, Broadway musicals, Spanish *zarzuelas,* and even Chinese-origin tunes in their *danzones.* See Carpentier, *La música,* 185.

13. The twentieth-century *danzón* orchestra consisted of flute, violins, piano, bass, and timbales. Modern *charangas* play the entire range of Cuban music and include conga drums and other percussion instruments in their ensembles.

14. Mario Bauzá, interview by Anthony Brown for Smithsonian Institution Jazz Oral History Program, September 9–10, 1992.

15. Rubén González would recall "Chanchullo" in the first few bars of "Tumbao," in his Buena Vista Social Club CD debut, *Introducing Rubén González,* in the late 1990s.

16. Initially called *sextetos* and then *septetos,* the *danzón* bands were dance groups that eventually included piano, bass, guitar, trumpet, voices, clave, maracas, and bongos. Modern *conjuntos* include conga drums, trumpets, trombones, and timbales.

17. See Roberts, *Latin Tinge,* chapter 4. The most famous rhumba in the 1930s was the Cuban *son* "The Peanut Vendor" (El manisero).

18. On the life and work of this unique artist, see Glenn Jacobs, "Cuba's Bola de Nieve: A Creative Looking Glass for Culture and the Artistic Self," *Latin American Music Review* 9, no. 1 (Spring/Summer 1988): 18–49.

19. Cachao played with the *charangas* of Marcelino González, Ernesto Muñoz, Antonio María Cruz, and Fernando Collazo.

20. Born in Cuba in 1904, Antonio Machín, a famed *sonero,* traveled to the United States in 1930 with the Don Aspiazu Orchestra. He recorded Cuban tunes with Mario Bauzá and popularized "The Peanut Vendor." In the late 1930s, he went to Europe on tour. Machín settled in Spain, where he helped popularize Cuban music. He died in Madrid in 1977.

21. A *tumbao* is rhythmic cell or unit for bass or conga, tied to the clave beat, which provides the basic building block of the syncopated structures of Cuban music. A *guajeo* is a melodic figure built upon the *tumbaos* of the bass and the conga, usually played by the violins in the *charanga* ensemble. It provides a syncopated background for the flute solos.

22. Up until the 1940s there was a clear separation in terms of the percussion instruments used by different ensembles. *Danzón charangas* employed timbales, *son* ensembles the bongos, while the congas *(tumbadoras)* were utilized in urban and rural rumba ensembles. In the mid-1930s, *son* groups—

which would subsequently be called *conjuntos*—began utilizing the sound of the conga. But adding the conga drum to complete a *conjunto* only took hold when Arsenio Rodríguez used it in 1940.

23. "Cachao: Mi idioma es un contrabajo," *El Espectador* (Bogotá), February 12, 1995.

24. As is often the case with successful innovations in popular styles, debates have occurred as to the invention of the mambo. I believe it is useful to see the appearance of the mambo as the result of the accumulated artistic endeavors of several key musicians including (besides Israel "Cachao" López) Orestes López, bandleader Antonio Arcaño, and the legendary Arsenio Rodríguez. The more dramatic innovations by Dámaso Pérez Prado have been acknowledged by everyone and especially by Cachao on several occasions. On this topic, see Radamés Giro, *El mambo* (Havana: Editorial Letras Cubanas, 1993); see also Cristóbal Díaz Ayala, *Música cubana: Del areíto a la nueva trova* (San Juan, Puerto Rico: Cubanacán, 1981); and Max Salazar, "Who Invented the Mambo," parts 1 and 2, *Latin Beat,* October 1992, 9–11, and November 1992, 9–12, respectively.

25. Israel "Cachao" López, interview for *Invention,* Discovery Channel, March 29, 1995.

26. Israel "Cachao" López, JOHP interview.

27. Milt Hinton, personal communication with author.

28. Israel "Cachao" López, JOHP interview.

29. "Cachao," *El Espectador,* February 12, 1995.

30. The musicians included, besides Cachao on bass (and piano in "Trombón criollo"), Orestes López, Generoso Jiménez, Alejandro Vivar, Guillermo Barretto, Tata Güines, Yeyito, Gustavo Tamayo, Emilio Peñalver, Virginio Lisama, Niño Rivera, and Richard Egües.

31. Pérez Prado always admired Cachao as a musician. See the testimony of Tite Curet Alonso, *La vida misma* (Caracas: M. J. Córdoba, 1993), 122.

32. Roberta Singer, "Tradition and Innovation in Contemporary Latin Popular Music in New York City," *Latin American Music Review* 4, no. 2 (1983): 183–202.

33. José de Córdoba, "Cuban Musical Legend Gets His Due," *Wall Street Journal,* August 26, 1992.

34. Roberto Hernández, *El Nacional,* November 27, 1994.

35. Romero, "Cachao."

36. Cuban recognition is best expressed in Carlos del Puerto and Silvio Vergara, *The True Cuban Bass* (Petaluma, CA: Sher Music Company, 1994).

Chapter Five

1. Some of the information for this chapter is based on a Smithsonian Institution Jazz Oral History Program (JOHP) interview conducted in New York City by the author with Mongo Santamaría on September 10 and 11, 1996.

2. For the most complete discography of the *son,* see Cristóbal Díaz Ayala, *Discografía de la música cubana,* vol. 1, *1898 a 1925* (San Juan, Puerto Rico: Fundación Musicalia, 1994).

3. Chicho worked in Mexico in the 1940s after traveling to Mexico City with an "Afro" show named *Batamú.* A notable bongo drummer, he was featured by Dámaso Pérez Prado in his recording of "Concierto para bongó."

4. On the history of the *Congo pantera* show, please see Leonardo Acosta, *Cubano Be, Cubano Bop,* mimeo (Havana: n.d), 150–53; see also Max Salazar, "Chano Pozo," *Latin Beat,* April 1993, 6–10.

5. Listen to Miguelito's improvisations on the conga in "José Isabel" by Electo "Chepín" Rosell or Beny Moré's lyrics in "Rumberos de ayer."

6. Chano Pozo was a prolific composer of many popular tunes such as "Anana Boroco Tinde," "Blen Blen Blen," "Parampampín," "Nagüe," "Guachi guaro," and others.

7. Santamaría, JOHP interview.

8. See José Manuel Gómez, *Guía esencial de la salsa* (Valencia: Editorial La Máscara, 1995).

9. Gómez, *Guía esencial,* 129.

10. Ibid.

Chapter Six

1. Some of the biographical data given in this chapter is drawn from a Smithsonian Jazz Oral History Program (JOHP) interview with Armando Peraza that I conducted with Anthony Brown. The interview took place in Foster City, CA, on September 29–30, 1994.

2. Guitarist, composer, and singer José Antonio Méndez, as a participant in the "feeling" movement, helped transform the Cuban bolero in the 1940s. Among his most notable boleros are "La gloria eres tú," "Novia mía," and "Ayer la vi llorar."

3. For information on the Ruta 23 and the entire complex of professional and amateur baseball in Cuba in the 1930s, see Roberto González Hecheva-

rría, *The Pride of Havana: A History of Cuban Baseball* (New York: Oxford University Press, 1999).

4. Peraza, JOHP interview.

5. Songwriter and bandleader Alberto Ruiz (1913–78) first appeared with the Sexteto Unión in 1928. In 1942, he organized the Conjunto Kubavana, which included Alejandro "Negro" Vivar on trumpet and vocalist Roberto Faz among its founders. See Helio Orovio, *Diccionario de la música cubana* (Havana: Editorial Letras Cubanas, 1992).

6. Rogelio Iglesias, known as "Yeyito," was one of the premiere bongo players in Havana in the 1930s, 1940s, and 1950s. He was a member of the Sexteto Sonora Nacional and later of the *conjunto* led by trumpeter Manolo Piñón. See Jesus Blanco Aguilar, *Ochenta años del son y los soneros del Caribe, 1909–1989* (Caracas: Fondo Editorial Tropykos, 1992).

7. Tata Güines, interview conducted by Radamés Giro, Héctor Corporán, and the author for the JOHP in Havana, January 5, 1999.

8. For information on the importance of this group in the history of the *son* in Mexico, see Merry Mac Masters, *Recuerdos del son* (Mexico: Consejo Nacional para la Cultura y las Artes, 1995); Rafael Figueroa Hernández, *Salsa mexicana: Transculturación e identidad* (Mexico City: ConClave, 1996).

9. Peraza, JOHP interview.

10. Max Salazar, "The Latin George Shearing," *Latin Beat,* February 1995, 32.

11. Trevor Salloum, *The Bongo Book* (Pacific, MO: Mel Bay Publications, 1997), 53.

12. Patato Valdés, JOHP interview, September 17, 1995, New York City.

13. Ibid.

14. Blanco Aguilar, *Ochenta Años,* 72.

15. See Max Salazar, "Arsenio Rodríguez: Life Was Like a Dream," *Latin Beat,* March 1994, 16.

16. See Orovio, *Diccionario,* 52.

17. Liner notes to CD *Patato Masterpiece,* Messidor, 1993.

18. Jesse Varela, "Patato: The Conguero with the Golden Hands," part 1, *Latin Beat,* April 1997, 45.

19. Jesse Varela, "Patato: The Conguero with the Golden Hands," part 2, *Latin Beat,* June/July 1997, 20–21.

20. For a complete discography on Patato Valdés, see Nat Chediak, *Diccionario del jazz latino* (Madrid: Fundación Auto, 1998).

21. Francisco Aguabella, interview by the author with Anthony Brown and Katherine Hagedorn for the JOHP, June 7–8, 1995, Beverly Hills, CA.

22. Ibid.

23. Jesse Varela, "Sworn to the Drum," *Latin Beat,* April 1994, 16–18.

24. Aguabella, JOHP interview.

25. Varela, "Sworn," part 2.

26. *La Opinión,* July 4, 1992.

27. Chediak, *Diccionario,* 53.

28. Max Salazar, "Salsa Hitmen," *Latin Beat,* February 1993, 24.

29. Salloum, *Bongo Book,* 54.

Chapter Seven

1. Some of the information in this chapter was obtained by the author at the Smithsonian Institution Jazz Oral History Program (JOHP) interview with Alfredo "Chocolate" Armenteros, September 9, 1996, in New York City.

2. Armando Armenteros became a successful trumpeter in Cuba before moving and settling in Spain. Another trumpeter, Alberto "Mazorca" Armenteros, who played for many years with the Conjunto Casino, was no relation to Chocolate.

3. Armenteros, JOHP interview.

4. The sound of "El Negro" Vivar can be heard in the famed 1957 *Descargas* by Cachao.

5. According to Leonardo Acosta, *Cubano Be, Cubano Bop,* mimeo (Havana, n.d.).

6. Cheo Marquetti, cousin of composer Luis Marquetti, was a great *reginero,* or singer of *guajiras.* He sang for the Orquesta Sensación and for the *charanga* of Cheo Belén Puig. Cheo Marquetti was the composer of the standard tune "Amor verdadero."

7. See Fabio Betancur Alvarez, *Sin clave y bongó no hay son* (Medellín: Editorial de la Universidad de Antioquia), 278–79.

Chapter Eight

1. Helio Orovio places Celia's birth in 1924. See his *Diccionario de la música cubana* (Havana: Editorial Letras Cubanas, 1992). However, indirect evidence

and oral testimonies based on conversations with Celia suggest an earlier date, probably 1920.

2. Celia Cruz, interview with the author and Anthony Brown for the Jazz Oral History Program (JOHP), Hollywood, CA, September 25–26, 1996.

3. Israel "Cachao" López remembered noticing Celia and her girlfriends dancing to the sounds of Arcaño, in Israel "Cachao" López, interview with the author and Anthony Brown for the JOHP, Miami, January 24–25, 1995.

4. See Umberto Valverde, *Celia Cruz: Reina rumba* (Bogotá: Arango Editores, 1995), 31.

5. As King of the contest, the jury selected Jesús Leyte, who sang the theme "Chivo que rompe tambó." In later years, Leyte would work as a vocalist for various groups, including Los Rivero. Cruz, JOHP interview. See also Fabio Betancur Alvarez, *Sin clave y bongó no hay son* (Medellín: Editorial Universidad de Antioquia, 1993).

6. Ayala, *Música cubana,* 148.

7. "Mango mangüé" was composed by Gilberto Valdés. Not to be confused with a tune by the same title authored by Francisco Fellove.

8. Cuban musicologist Leonardo Acosta shares the widely held opinion that Cuban popular music could reasonably be divided into two periods, before and after the appearance of radio station Mil Diez. See Acosta, *Cubano Be, Cubano Bop,* chap. 3.

9. Bobby Collazo, *La última noche que pasé contigo* (San Juan, Puerto Rico: Editorial Cubanacán, 1987), 233.

10. The phrase comes from Delfín Moré, brother of Beny Moré, in a documentary made in Cuba in the 1970s.

11. Bebo Valdés is an outstanding figure in modern Cuban popular music. He composed several hits, including "Rareza del siglo," and created the *batanga* rhythm. Bebo Valdés was a leading musician in the development of Afro-Cuban jazz in 1950s Havana and is the father of another salient figure in Cuban music, Chucho Valdés.

12. See Raúl Fernández, "La magia musical de Cachao," *Huellas, Revista de la Universidad del Norte* 44 (1995): 3–13.

13. Indeed, musicians from these and other groups were very critical of the Sonora Matancera style, which was derided as "easy music" and "music for whites."

14. Among the better-known ensembles are the Sonora Santanera, the Sonora Dinamita, and the Sonora Ponceña. Many *sonoras* appeared in Colombia: Antillana, del Caribe, Tropical, Silver, Curro, Cordobesa, and others. A

number of radio programs entirely dedicated to the Sonora Matancera have been regularly broadcast in various Colombian cities over several decades. In Medellín, a group of enthusiasts founded the Club Social y Cultural Sonora Matancera. The reader interested in a detailed history of the Sonora Matancera should consult Héctor Ramírez Bedoya, *Historia de la Sonora Matancera y sus estrellas* (Medellín: Editorial Impresos Begón, 1996). For a critical analysis of the Sonora Matancera's music, see Alejandro Ulloa, *La salsa en Cali* (Cali: Ediciones Universidad del Valle, 1992), 140–48.

15. During this period, she appeared in the following movies: *Olé Cuba, Una gallega en La Habana, Rincón criollo, Piel canela,* and *An Affair in Havana.*

16. Cruz, JOHP interview. See also Betancur Alvarez, *Sin clave,* 265–66.

17. The phrase is Paquito D'Rivera's, in *Como su ritmo no hay dos,* a documentary by Andy Garcia, Cineson, 1993.

18. José Arteaga, *La salsa* (Bogotá: Intermedio Editores, 1990), 52–53.

19. Pacheco's father had been director of the Orquesta Santa Cecilia in Santiago de los Caballeros. The famous merengue "Compadre Pedro Juan," composed by the orchestra's pianist, Luis Alberti, was first recorded by the Orquesta Santa Cecilia.

20. Her roles as a *santero*'s mother in *The Mambo Kings* and as a spiritualist in *The Perez Family* have strengthened the public's belief that Celia Cruz was a devotee of Santería, a suggestion she denied in our JOHP interview.

21. Celia has sung duets with a large number of other distinguished vocalists, including Beny Moré, Johnny Ventura, Dyango, and Caetano Veloso, among others.

22. For the Beatles tribute she recorded "Obladi, Oblada." Her favorite Beatles tune has always been "Yesterday," which she sang live at the El Zorro in Acapulco (Cruz, JOHP interview).

23. Ayala, *Música cubana.*

24. Sometimes nicknames and geography can be at odds; in much of South America, Celia Cruz, who was born in Havana (on the western part of the island), is called the Guarachera de Oriente (referring to the eastern part of Cuba).

INDEX

Compositor:	Sheridan Books
Text:	11/15 Granjon
Display:	Granjon
Index:	Barbara Roos
Printer/Binder:	Sheridan Books